How to Raise an AMERICAN PATRIOT

Making it Okay for Our Kids to Be Proud to Be American

MARIJO N. TINLIN

NEW YORK

How to Raise an AMERICAN PATRIOT
MAKING IT OKAY FOR OUR KIDS
TO BE PROUD TO BE AMERICAN
by Marijo N. Tinlin

ISBN 978-1-60037-950-5 PB
ISBN 978-1-60037-951-2 EB
Library of Congress Control Number: 2011924967

Published by:

Morgan James Publishing

The Entrepreneurial Publisher
5 Penn Plaza, 23rd Floor
New York City, New York 10001
(212) 655-5470 Office
(516) 908-4496 Fax
www.MorganJamesPublishing.com

Cover Design by:
Rachel Lopez
rachel@r2cdesign.com

Interior Design by:
Bonnie Bushman
bbushman@bresnan.net

In an effort to support local communities, raise awareness and funds, Morgan James Publishing donates one percent of all book sales for the life of each book to Habitat for Humanity.

Get involved today, visit
www.HelpHabitatForHumanity.org.

ACKNOWLEDGMENTS

This book could never have been written without the help of a multitude of people. I knew almost none of the contributors to this book so I had to activate every avenue of my network. Without these people, this book would not exist.

My eternal gratitude goes to:

My husband, Steve, without whom I would never have had the courage to write this.

My kids—little patriots in the making, we hope—Jackson, Brooke, and John, and my stepsons, Andy and Adam. You make us proud and also teach us a lot about ourselves.

My mom, Mary Lou Newton, my confidant when I wasn't totally sure this book would happen. You kept my secret. Love to you, Mother, and thank you for everything.

Joel Comm, owner of Family First (www.familyfirst.com), the site which I edit, thank you for your connections and for getting my career as a journalist back in action. Your confidence in my efforts gave me strength, and my "editor" title, gave me more credibility.

David Hancock, at Morgan James, for taking a chance on me and my idea. Judi Moss, my editor and Susan Burgess from eTranscriptionSolutions for helping me make this book better. Katie Kaplan, and the Nelson Family — Elisabeth, Allie and Peter for babysitting! Amity Cooper, Stacey Kannenberg, Kimbirly Orr, Christi Johnson, Kimberly Mazza, Kathy Hall, Chris Castilian, Emily Leibert, Jessica Derksen, Shannon Donnelly, Eileen Parker, Sharon Silver, Rob James and Amy Foster for their help, advice, guidance and connections.

To all the contributors—thank you for having faith in me to tell your personal story adequately and for knowing how important being an American Patriot really is.

To our Founding Fathers for their wisdom, bravery and perseverance.

And to God for the little voice in my heart that kept me going, even when I was discouraged. Thank you for sending me the idea and giving me the strength to pursue it.

TABLE OF CONTENTS

INTRODUCTION
★ ★ ★ ★ ★

"If American liberty loses its luster, the dimming will come from within. It will be due to our own lack of attention and devotion. Without patriotism, there cannot be a United States. It falls upon us—upon you and me—to take care of this miraculous American democracy, to make it work, to *love* it." (Dr. William J. Bennett and John T.E. Cribb, page xii Introduction, *The American Patriot's Almanac*)

As parents, we are the role models for our children, our future. We show them what it's like to love (or hate). Expressions of love come in different forms—love of parents, love of a spouse, love of siblings, family and friends, and love of country.

When we talk about how our government victimizes, terrorizes, conquers and destroys, we show our kids that this land is a land of hate. People at the highest levels of our own government have spent significant time apologizing to those who wish to hurt us. Maybe it's because they believe we should not be the leader in the world.

That's not what is going to keep us great.

Showing our children what is strong about our nation, why we are the greatest nation, and who fought to bring this greatness and opportunity to them—that's how we show our love for this nation. That's how we express our pride and love of country.

Teaching our children to pledge allegiance, not blindly, but out of pride for a country so grand, so divinely inspired that we added the words "under God" to our Pledge of Allegiance only 60 years ago. That's what teaches them about why we are exceptional, why we truly are the "shining city upon the hill" as President Ronald Reagan famously referenced in his farewell speech.

Teaching about the Founding Fathers, the men who lost their homes, property, families and, in many cases, their lives, so that we can live in the Land of the Free and the Home of the Brave. These are the stories that spark that flame of patriotism in a child's heart.

Do your kids think about these things? Probably not.

Why not? Because there's a good chance they don't even know about the struggles our founders endured for them, because many of our schools spend very little time on this subject. I guarantee you, when your children do learn, after you teach them, they will have a new found appreciation for their own freedom, the price of freedom and the long-lasting effect it has. I've seen this light dawn in my own children's eyes.

They will stop fixating on all the *victims* they learn about in school every day—the slaves, the oppressed, the victims of civil rights violations. They will start thinking about having pride in themselves, in their families, in their country and its history.

They might even make the ultimate choice as a patriot by putting their own lives on the line by joining the military. Putting themselves in harm's way just like our founders did, so that others might be free, and sleep soundly at night, never wondering if they would wake to the sound of gunfire or explosions.

They most likely will never come to these conclusions on their own. You, as a parent, must help them discover these things within themselves, as individuals.

This book gives you, the parents, the tools you need to start your children, grandchildren, cousins, nieces and nephews, down the pathway of true and deep pride in our country. Through the words of 13 patriots profiled within these pages, you will hear what patriotism is about. You will learn how these patriots were raised, what they have done to raise their own patriots and what suggestions they give to you about how to raise your own patriot.

Their words will help you instill in your children the wisdom of our founders and the devotion so many have to this beautiful, divine country we have the privilege to call "home."

In his introduction to *The American Patriot's Almanac,* Bill Bennett wrote these perfect words: "If the United States is not worth loving, then no country is." He wrote, "Nobody wants the United States to be a republic of sheep. We need, in James Madison's own words, a nation of 'loving critics' who use their free minds and free wills to examine the country's actions closely and raise concerns when necessary."

In recent years, some "loving critics" have gotten quite a bit of attention. This is why so much attention is being paid to the Tea Party movement. The giant awoke. It started to make noise.

National pride soared almost a decade ago when President George W. Bush, dressed in a flight suit, jumped down from a fighter jet that landed on the *USS Abraham Lincoln* as it returned from its combat mission in the Persian Gulf. We needed that pride after the horror of September 11, 2001. We need that again.

And no book about this great country's founding and principles would be complete without the mention of divine inspiration and providence. When you read *Red State* Editor Erick Erickson's profile, he references 1864 as a year that turned the tide for the Civil War. He also mentions his discussions with Vice President Dick Cheney and *The Weekly Standard* Executive Editor, Fred Barnes, about this specific year, and how, without divine intervention, the war would have turned another way and our nation may have fallen.

Jackie Gingrich Cushman mentions that President Lincoln was waiting for a sign from God to deliver the Gettysburg Address. He got it via the Battle of Antietam. She also mentions the incredible events that happened to General George Washington during the Revolutionary War—his horses being shot out from underneath him, bullets flying through his clothes, but not hitting him—as examples that God had a plan for General Washington, and He watched over him to make sure this plan was carried out.

Without some level of faith in a higher being, understanding this great nation's past and potential is difficult. The phrase "In God We Trust" is deliberately printed on our currency as a reminder of our founding. We must trust in God that our country will stay great in perpetuity.

In these pages, you will hear the words of 13 patriots who are also sons and daughters, parents, even grandparents. They all have very different backgrounds and life experiences. Not all are household names, but their intent and purpose all serve one goal—to raise good patriots.

I'm proud to say I spoke to each of them, listened to their stories, and was honored to hear about a small slice of their lives. I am privileged to write their words and give you their thoughts about what they learned as children, what influenced them as individuals, and what they have done or are doing to influence their children now.

Within each chapter, the contributors give their suggestions and tips to parents about how to raise good patriots, by speaking to them about fundamental principles such as duty, sovereignty and heritage.

It's interesting that no two people had exactly the same advice, but many mention common themes. For example, political pundit Kevin Jackson, author/pundit Rachel Campos-Duffy and author/columnist Jackie Gingrich Cushman, all mention that you don't have to be born in this country to be a patriot and love our country. Hilldale College president, Dr. Larry Arnn, and the Reverend Steven Craft, both mention that we must teach our children to seek truth, not simply allow them to form their opinion of truth. Campos-Duffy and Cushman also agree that most kids understand much more than we give them credit for, and that we shouldn't underestimate their ability to grasp the concepts we want to discuss with them.

Each one of the participants has his or her own opinion, which does not necessarily reflect the opinions of the others in this book, this author, or the publisher of this book. But as a collective, all the participants have the same thing in common—a great love of our country and for its founding principles.

This book is about teaching your children to be their own people, no matter where they come out on the scale—right, left, moderate, whatever. You simply need to encourage them to think for themselves, to be their own people, and to understand the great opportunity living in this country allows for them.

I hope what you read in this book helps you learn more about our country, and I hope you pass this along to your own mini-patriots so we can keep our Republic strong, our faith unwavering, and our flag flying proudly forever.

Chapter 1

TRUTH

Dr. Larry Arnn

★ ★ ★ ★ ★

Dr. Larry Arnn has been the 12th president of Hillsdale College in Hillsdale, Michigan since May 2000. He is a member of the board of directors for The Heritage Foundation, The Claremont Institute and the Henry Salvatori Center of Claremont McKenna College. He is also the author of *Liberty and Learning: The Evolution of American Education*, published by Hillsdale College Press in 2004. He and his wife, Penelope, have four children.

Arnn talks about his early influences in his life—his early love of history and his family's involvement in the military and how that brought him to love this country.

"My dad was a school teacher," he says, "and he and his brothers all served in the military. My dad was of an age where he was about to get sent to the Pacific front in the Second World War when the war ended. His two younger brothers went to Korea. One was killed there and another wounded. My father was both mournful and proud at the loss of his brother; he could not bear to hear Taps played, as it reminded him of it. He and his brothers were proud to think that people from Arkansas were good soldiers, patriotic and dutiful. Service to the country was a big thing.

"I developed a love of history when I was a boy. I read a lot of history books when I was growing up, and I used to talk to my dad about that a lot. I loved the story of Bunker Hill; how the British tried to walk down the road and we hid behind the trees and shot them. I remember rehearsing that story with my dad. It was an adventure story. I grew up around patriotic people who thought they ought to be of service to their country."

As an educator, Arnn knows how humans learn. Here he tells us how that process happens in young people and why this process must happen for kids to come to their own conclusions about being a good patriot.

"Kids learn a lot from watching," Arnn says. "Their education is happening inside them. There are a lot of things more fundamental than patriotism that have to be learned in order for patriotism to develop in the right way. I do not think you can make it develop directly.

"First, kids need to grow up in a world where they think things are real. Many people today think that everything is according to perspective, that everybody has his own perspective. Kids are taught that every time and place has its own perspective, and the great thing is to understand that and cultivate your own perspective, whatever you may wish it to be.

"Ask a kid, 'What is your favorite subject?' And they will say, 'Politics.' 'History.' 'English.' Then ask them, 'What is that?' Come to find out, it is hard to answer that question. You have to think for a long time to name the essential attributes of any complex thing. Young people have a short cut: They look at it as a matter of perspective. They will ask, 'Whose opinion do you want?' A good thing to reply is, 'I do not really want an opinion. I am wondering what *it* is.' If we could know what it is, then we could know whether the opinions about it have any value.

"Sometimes students here at the college will say, 'If I come to Hillsdale, are you going to respect my opinion?' And I say, 'No, we do not really care about that.' We would like rather to know the truth, and that means we have a lot of work to do. That means we all argue that through and figure it out. We need to direct young people outside themselves, because the thinking at their age tends to make their understanding collapse upon itself. You have to get that inside thinking out of them, because it will compromise their ability to learn.

"I'll give you another illustration. In the *AP Guide for English Literature*, the introduction says that in teaching English, we used to privilege the text over the reader, but now, objectivity and factuality are out the door. Now, it says, we teach students to find their own reality in the text, no doubt hoping that they will discover values to guide them through a mad, mad world.

"What that means is in English class, we do not teach the kids that the book is anything real. If you read Shakespeare's play, the point is not the play or what Shakespeare is saying, or still less, the nature that Shakespeare is describing. Instead, the point is what you think about it. If young people grow up thinking like that, then when Thomas Jefferson says that the country is founded according to the laws of Nature and of Nature's God, they do not think that is anything, and that deprives the American Revolution of its dignity.

"When I thought about those war stories from the Revolution, I was a little boy in Arkansas, and I thought those Minutemen were people like me. I thought these soldiers with their fancy coats and their wigs, coming from a king, were hoity-toity people. I thought, it is not right for hoity-toity people to tell the other people what to do just because they want to. In other words, I believed all men are created equal, but that means that I believed that there is such a thing as a man. Man is not just something in my imagination, he is a real thing, and he is different from a pig.

"That is an incredibly significant point in the history of the country. In one of the Lincoln-Douglas Debates about taking the slaves into the federal territories and having your property guaranteed in them, Stephen Douglas says, 'Lincoln says I can take my hog or my buckboard into Nebraska, and the federal government will protect my property in it, but he will not say the same thing for my slave. That is not consistent.' And Lincoln says, 'It is inconsistent if there is no difference between the hog and the slave, but you know the difference. The people in the South have never passed a law to try a pig for murder, or making it illegal to teach a pig to read.'"

Finding truth outside of one's perception of reality is the key to understanding anything as real, according to Dr. Arnn. He says so much of what children are exposed to today is not real, including television, video games, and on-line relationships. We must first help them understand reality. Then they will understand truth and the significance of the American Revolution in our history, which leads to patriotism.

"The first thing is reality," Dr. Arnn continues. "Kids need to know reality. They need to know that a profound understanding of it is incredibly difficult to get, but they have to trust their senses, and they have to develop their understanding. As Aristotle writes, 'There is nothing in the soul that does not get there through the senses.' Our contact with the outside world is through our senses. Are the things that

we see real? Are our perceptions of them real? If you think that they are
not, then the argument between the King of England and the founders
of America is just one arbitrary claim against another. But, if you think
they are real, then there can be such things as Laws of Nature and there
can be natural and equal rights, because there is nature.

"The first step is to teach them that everything in the world that
they see is real, and their challenge is to understand it. Just that fact will
make them better students, because now they have something valuable
to be doing in school and in their studies. But then, the second thing is
to teach them that claims of justice - of right and wrong - are extremely
important. In fact, 'Making those claims and asking questions about
those claims,' writes Aristotle, 'is a specific human gift. It is what we do
that beasts do not do.'

"The claims of justice made by the United States of America are real
statements about things that are real. You can compare those statements
to the real things, and see if they are true and beautiful. Then, you can
attach a loyalty to the country because you see that it is good and true
and beautiful. That is really fundamental to educating a kid. We are in a
time when going back to these fundamental claims that are made in the
American Revolution and evaluating those again and seeing the truth or
the merit of the claim is the key to restoring patriotism."

Dr. Arnn points out that the real way to teach a child to own their
thoughts is through a thorough examination of claims for and against
something. Then an educated conclusion, based in truth, can be found.

"Around here," he says, "sometimes we are congratulated, because
Hillsdale College is a big old argument. We love the Constitution here.
We teach it like nobody. Well, half the readings in the *Constitution Reader*
are written by people who are *against* the Constitution. Of course they
are, because that is the story. The only way to teach anybody anything
is by examining the claims about it. The question of orthodoxy does

not come up until you have gotten somewhere in the examination. The point is, the way you make an orthodox thinker is by a real examination of the claims. Then it can be their own understanding and not just something they are repeating because somebody said it to them.

"My children have grown up in a time when they need reasons. They need real knowledge, because everything is contested. If you start them on the track and make that kind of learning available to them, they do the work. I did not really understand it until I started teaching a lot. If all you do is tell students what to think, they can get that in a hurry, and they are thinking, 'What is next?' They put that on a shelf in their mind somewhere and think, 'I will figure out later if I am going to think that.' Whereas, if you make them go through the arguments, that is intoxicating and difficult and demanding, and then things become their own.

"One of the points then is you have to raise up thinking human beings, but not with the idea that they should think whatever they want to think. They have to think what is true, and that means they have to make a case for it.

"Thomas Jefferson and James Madison left specific advice about how to make people patriotic. That advice was they should read the story of their country. If they are going to be leaders, they should read the great books, and they gave a list of those great books.[1] In the end, that is the

---

1   Per Dr. Arnn, this particular list of books was given in the correspondence between Jefferson and Madison in discussing the proper study for the law classes at the University of Virginia. On February 8, 1825, Madison wrote to Jefferson, agreeing with the list of proposed works: "And on the distinctive principles of the Government of our own State, and of that of the U. States, the best guides are to be found in – 1. The Declaration of Independence, as the fundamental act of Union of these States. 2. the book known by the title of the 'Federalist,' being an authority to which appeal is habitually made by all and rarely declined or denied by any, as evidence of the general opinion of those who framed and those who accepted the Constitution of the U. States on questions as to its genuine meaning. 3. the Resolutions of the General Assembly of Virgᵃ in 1799, on the subject of the Alien and Sedition laws, which appeared to accord with the predominant sense of the people of the U. S. 4. The Inaugural Speech and Farewell Address of President Washington, as conveying political lessons of peculiar value; and that in the branch of the School of law which is to treat on the subject of Govt, these shall be used as the text and documents of the School."(*The Republic of Letters: The Correspondence between Thomas Jefferson and James Madison 1776-1826*. James Morton Smith, ed. New York: W. W. Norton & Co., 1995. Vol. 3, pp. 1924-26.)

way, especially in a controversial time like this. You have to start back at the beginning and build up."

Two of Arnn's children are currently attending Hillsdale and his oldest graduated from another small liberal arts college and is now working on a Ph.D., so they are learning or have learned to think through issues in this way and come to their own conclusions about things, including their country. .

Arnn also discusses why it is important for kids to understand politics. Being political is part of our nature as humans. To understand is what makes us true citizens. "Kids today think that politics is optional," he says. "It is like that old saying, 'You may not be interested in war, but war is very interested in you.' They need to know that politics is very interested in them. Aristotle's account of the human being is a synonym for the faculty of speech. You could not talk if you could not reason and to be reasonable is to be able to speak. He puts this argument together in about three pages, and it is very beautiful how he does it. It takes a little bit of understanding, but what it proves is human beings are unique, because they have this gift of reason. They can use common nouns. That makes them able to speak, which makes them social, moral, and therefore, political.

"Human beings live under law. They always do. They always will so long as they are human beings, and it is definitive for them whether the law is good or not. Every thinking human being has a keen interest in politics as a citizen. You need to teach young people that. They need to know that. All of my kids know that. They may not like it. My elder son does not want to be involved in politics much, but he understands it is mandatory upon him that he behaves as a citizen, because he knows what his nature is.

"For the young, it changes the game when you prove that to them. We are dealing with fourteen hundred students at a time here at Hillsdale every year. It is amazing what you learn from that, because of course, you have failures. And the failures say, 'I do not care about politics.' That means there is something they missed. They do not know it, but it is their nature to care about and to be involved in politics. It is going to affect them."

In discussing how he taught his children about the founding documents, he points out that three of the four have attended a school where the Constitution and other founding documents are taught. In his house, they are often a topic of discussion.

"In our house, there is a fair amount of knowledge about the meaning of the United States, so they grew up around that. And also, in my family, we always took the kids to conferences and events. When the kids were little, I would get a couple of hotel rooms and we would all stay together. They would come to the dinner and they would hear what was said. They had their kid way of listening, which involved a lot of making fun of it, including of their dad. But that also means they heard.

"You have to teach them that what they think is the ultimate test, and the way you pass that test is make an argument. It has to be true. It had to be good. It has to stand up and be more truthful than the counter arguments. Just because it is their own does not give it any dignity at all.

"Once my son said to me, 'Dad, do you expect me to agree with you?' I said, 'Goodness, son, I can't even agree with myself half the time.' I said, 'Why don't you just try to get it right?' And I could see him relax. That was a big thing with him. He has to be a man. I do not think anything that I do not have to justify. He is in the same boat.

"All of my kids grew up in a household where people are knowledgeable about politics and they grew up in a world where it is not all that cool to talk about it all the time. Young people do not do that unless they are nerdy.

"Here at Hillsdale College, we have factions gathered around the core curriculum. The English majors think the great books, the beautiful books, the poems and the epics and the novels and the plays are the thing. Others think philosophy is the thing. And the political science students think politics is the thing. The reason the factions do not become virulent, and they do not usually, is because there is a core curriculum. Everybody has to take all that stuff. The position of the college is that the subjects within the core curriculum are aspects of a whole. We are here to build a picture together of what the whole is, and politics is included in that whole.

"So, when my kids are around this town, they are in a world where that is what people think. They have all the normal reactions kids here at Hillsdale do that other kids do. 'I do not like politics.' 'I do not like history.' 'I do not like chemistry.' It doesn't matter whether you like it or not. It is a real thing. You are going to have to know something about it.

"The truth is the kids are too young. When you are 19, it is too early to know a lot of things; you have to dig. Get them to dig, to build in them the spirit to want to dig, if they do not already have it. And it is in there. You do not really build it; you just ignite it or open it up. Give them something to dig into.

"So, about being a proud American, my kids are all that. They are all unreserved about that. Good for them. Bless them. I do not think it is because I did anything specific. It is because I did all this. And much more important than what I did, is what they did. Some kids want to dig more than others and they tend to be better students."

Arnn's advice for parents on how to raise a patriot includes reading the history and the source documents and then letting them think for themselves.

"I would work through the *Constitution Reader* of Hillsdale College," Arnn says. "It starts with Aristotle. That means you can find out what it is to be a human being. Once you know that, politics is a thing you can define. It is the highest Earthly form of human community, and human beings naturally form communities. Once you know that, then you take up the study of your country in the way that Thomas Jefferson or James Madison did. They knew the definition of politics when they started. The second thing is to read the Declaration of Independence and try to figure out what it says. You are on your way if you just do those two simple things. Everybody can read those documents."

Hillsdale's *Constitution Reader* and the Declaration of Independence teach kids about being patriots, and teaching itself is an expression of patriotism, in Arnn's opinion.

"The kids should learn. They should learn the value of learning English. They should learn what they are. They should learn what their country is. If they really do learn those things, the chances of them rejecting that are small."

★ ★ ★ *Key Points* ★ ★ ★

- Seek truth, not just a perception of truth by "seeking the essential attributes," or nature, of a thing, instead of a perspective about it.

- Teach your children how to think logically for themselves so they can make educated decisions and not be misled by others.

- Read the Hillsdale *Constitution Reader* and Declaration of Independence with them and discuss what they mean.

- Do not tell them what to think. Discuss with them why they think what they think and have them make an argument.

Chapter 2

PRIDE

Rachel Campos-Duffy

★ ★ ★ ★ ★

Rachel Campos-Duffy is the mother of 6 children with her husband, Wisconsin Representative Sean Duffy. The two met while filming one of the first reality shows, "The Real World: San Francisco." She is also a political pundit, blogger, and author of *Stay Home, Stay Happy—10 Secrets to Loving At-Home Motherhood.* At times, she fills in as the conservative voice on "The View."

She discusses how having pride in our country and not being afraid to show it really exhibits patriotism. She encourages parents to tell our kids about current events, and engage them in the process of government and civics, and teach them about American history. These things help raise patriots.

Campos-Duffy talks about the influence of her parents on her upbringing as an American patriot. Rachel's mother became a citizen after marrying Rachel's father. They met while he was stationed in Spain, her native country.

"She's the most patriotic person I know. She loves America. Everything from bigger washing machines and Disneyland to the freedom, liberties and opportunities America offers."

Rachel's father is Mexican-American and was one of 15 kids. "My dad grew up dirt-poor in the mountains of Arizona," she says.

"He came from a union copper mining town where you either worked for the copper mining company or you joined the military. He joined the military. He was a Democrat, but the first Republican he ever voted for was Ronald Regan, and he's never gone back. He voted for Reagan because, as a military man, he understood first-hand the dangers abroad. At the time, the military was in disrepair and it wasn't being funded sufficiently. Reagan was a vote for a stronger and better America.

"As he got older, my father also became more appreciative of the opportunities America offered. He went into the military, and earned his Bachelor's Degree while he served. He left the military, earned his Master's degree, and became a teacher.

"His four children have gone on to get higher degrees and are living the American Dream. In addition, like most Hispanics, my dad is socially conservative and he believes that the GOP is the natural home for a conservative Catholic.

"Being an Hispanic Republican is not the dichotomy the media portrays. If you ask Hispanics whether hard work should be rewarded, about the importance of personal responsibility, opposition to abortion, and their views on traditional marriage they are clearly social conservatives. They feel at home in the GOP. And on both fiscal and social issues and in their pride for America, my parents are clearly "Tea Partiers." They were Tea Partiers before Tea Partiers were cool. When I think back on it, it really was amazing how much they embraced American exceptionalism and passed that love of America on to their children.

"Growing up, my parents wanted us to see the historical sites in America. Nowadays, it might seem hokey to take a family road trip to go see The Liberty Bell, or Constitution Hall, but these were things that we did growing up."

Now, as a parent to six children, Campos-Duffy talks about how she and her husband are trying to instill a love of country in their own children.

"It's like so many other things in parenting, where we underestimate our kids. We assume they're only going to love Disneyland or Sea World. And yet, when you take your kids to historical sites, they clearly enjoy it. My kids absolutely loved Williamsburg and Jamestown, for example.

"If we want our kids to get excited about American history, we really should make the effort to show them some history. Take that road trip! Go old-school! Your kids will look back on those memories with fondness and pride."

With her husband's recent campaign, her children were able to experience the democratic process first-hand by helping out. Campos-Duffy talks about her kids' involvement, and how great she feels about them getting involved early in their lives.

"Our kids rollerblade in parades, pass out literature for their dad, and stuff envelopes for the campaign.

"I wasn't involved with campaigns until college, but my kids are getting this experience in pre-school and grade school. I understand that not every child's parent is going to run for Congress, but the children are also realizing how much work, and how many volunteers it takes to run a campaign. Mom and Dad can't do this alone and there is a way for citizens to participate at every level.

"They can see first-hand that everybody counts. If we didn't have people to walk in a parade with us, it would be a very lonely campaign and we'd probably lose! I never cease to be impressed and humbled by the time people take out of their busy lives to help a candidate and a campaign. The people who show up at 9 AM to walk in a parade with their families are modeling the same civic example as we are doing for our kids. Your parent doesn't have to run for office to experience this process. Our political system is awesome and everybody has a place and a part to play. That's really what is so unique about America."

She talks about how political involvement, even at the earliest age, can influence a child.

"Knowing my kids are getting this kind of exposure to the political process at such a tender age makes me wonder what they'll be doing in junior high or high school."

Rachel says that there are politicians who make a point of keeping their kids out of the spotlight for fear of them being overshadowed by their parents or the campaign.

"I see it differently and maybe because we are so new to all of this. I wouldn't want to deny my kids a front seat to this process.

"Yes, it's true that kids can often take a back seat to a political event or especially the last few weeks of a campaign. But I'm not sure that that is so bad. Kids ought to know they're not always the center of the universe. In fact, I think it's good for kids to see that there are things that are bigger than us. There's a whole country trying to get back on track. There are moments that supersede what you want to do at that particular moment.

"Before we jumped into the race, we sat down with our kids and we talked to them about what was going on in the country. We told them, 'This is going to be really hard. There are going to be days when you don't like it and you wish Dad was home, but if this is what we believe we need to do this as a family.' They all agreed that they wanted their dad to do take on this challenge.

"When they complained during the campaign (and they did!), we reminded them, 'Remember when we had that meeting and you guys said you wanted Dad to do something about all that stuff?' 'Oh yeah..' they would say.

"We got them involved at the ground level and they've had to make sacrifices along with us. We tell them that that's their part of giving back to the country."

Asked what her kids would say about being an American patriot and how much they love their country, Rachel gives two examples of how much her kids really understand.

"No kid should know this much about the stimulus package! When we told them about the debt, they were horrified that we were passing this debt on to them; they were like, 'You gotta do something, Dad. We don't want to have to pay that back. It's not fair!' It's funny how they just got it!

"One of the other ways we bring appreciation for the United States to our children is to contrasts the U.S. with other countries. They benefit from knowing how we live versus other nations. For example, I have clipped articles about the way girls are treated in China or the Middle East and talked to my kids about that. I am NOT afraid to say to my kids, 'You live in the best country in the world!' A lot of people don't like to say that. I have absolutely no bones about it. I just say, 'You are the luckiest person to live in this country.'

"There are opportunities in every current event conversation a parent has with a child to talk about those differences and to bring out pride in America. I think there's a tendency to shy away from that because it seems too prideful or arrogant. I don't know what's going on in our country these days, but I don't shy away telling my kids how great this country is."

Rachel has some additional advice for parents as they try and raise their own patriots.

"Too often, we underestimate what children are capable of understanding or sitting through. There is no substitute for taking your kid to a rally, a Tea Party, a city hall meeting. Those are very educational experiences that enforce our need to participate in our system of government and just how great our country is."

Asked what values being a patriot instills in children, Campos-Duffy says "Pride." Her daughter won a competition in 2010 through the website Constituting America, which has the purpose of helping Americans learn about the importance of the Constitution and other founding documents. This contest really helped her further develop pride in her country and in the Constitution.

"The Constituting America contest was such a great opportunity. She read about the Constitution and the founding fathers before she sat down to draw. We talked about our rights coming from God and the proper role of government. In the end, all of our kids learned more by listening to the discussions we had with her about her plans for her drawing. When these kinds of opportunities come up, it's important as parents to encourage our kids to participate."

★ ★ ★ *Key Points* ★ ★ ★

- You don't have to be born in America to be a patriot.

- Visit historical sites.

- Talk to your children about current events.

- Don't underestimate what your kids will understand.

- Get children involved in their community government for first-hand experience.

- Don't be afraid to show your pride in our country—it rubs off on your kids.

★ ★ ★ ★ ★

Chapter 3

SOVEREIGNTY

The Reverend Steven Craft

The Reverend Steven Louis Craft holds a Master of Divinity Degree from Harvard Divinity School in Cambridge, Massachusetts. He is a former prison chaplain and is the Executive Director of Christian Citizenship Ministries, Inc. He is the co-author of *Virtue and Vice: A Fascinating Journey into Spiritual Transformation* and the author of *Morality and Freedom: America's Dynamic Duo*. Besides being a member of the Constitution Party, he is also a national speaker for the John Birch Society. He is married and has a son, a daughter and two stepdaughters.

Craft talks about the early childhood influences that inspired his strong love of country.

"I'm 67. I've been around for a few minutes. I am a black American clergyperson patriot. I grew up during the Jim Crow segregation era in the United States. In my tradition, the black tradition, growing up during a time of overt segregation and racism, a lot of people in my generation were very angry and bitter about their American heritage. I had to learn that, even though we were held down by racism and oppression, America was the greatest country in the world. I learned that, even though America had her problems, America was the greatest nation on the planet. That's the way I was raised."

Reverend Craft is very concerned about the state of our country and how the nation's youth are not being taught about preserving our sovereignty, but to think of the world as one community and disparage their American heritage. He thinks this thinking is *extremely* dangerous and that it must be stopped and brought back to our founding principles.

"As a motivational speaker and minister, when I talk to my people and they bash America, I ask them, 'Where else would you go? We're the only place on the planet where you can go from being penniless or homeless to becoming a multi-millionaire.'

"We've seen the humongous advances black people have made from the time we were brought over here on slave ships. We have black billionaires. We have black millionaires. We have middle class people and those in poverty.

"My message now, when I'm on the speaking circuit and when I'm writing books, is to tell our people and all Americans there is no country on Planet Earth that is better than the United States. If one does not love our nation, then one needs to leave.

"We now have forces that are working against our country, forces that are determined to bring us into bondage, totalitarianism, atheism, communism, working to destroy our country.

"One of the things God has put into my heart is to really speak against these things and to raise-up a standard with young people, to get people to see that we've got to get back to some basic patriotic and American principles.

"If you're born in America, you're an American citizen and you thank God for America. America has problems; what nation doesn't? If you don't like America, go to North Korea or Nigeria or Venezuela or Cuba.

"I don't see anybody trying to get out of Dodge. I don't see anybody leaving America. I see everybody trying to get in here. I see everybody trying to jump over the fence illegally, or cross ocean waters on rickety boats.

"I don't see anybody getting out of America, but I see all these people *bashing* America. There's a reason for that—there are satanic forces working to destroy our nation, because our nation truly is the last great bastion of hope.

"It's going to take a whole lot more than teaching these young people, who have a post-modern collective mindset of thinking that socialism and communism and all of these other ideologies, ungodly theologies, are going to work. It's going to take more than that to turn this mess around.

"For example, I did a talk the other day in a school, and now the buzz phrase in that school was 'global citizen.' 'It takes a village to raise a child.' Well, when we grew-up there was no such thing as that, because it's a lie. It takes a mom and a dad to raise a child, not the Village of Monroe Township in New Jersey.

"Everything now is turned upside down. Things that we learned that were common sense principles—love of God, love of country, strong families—all that now is being kicked to the curb. We believe in global citizenship, sustainable development, communism, Marxism, men marrying men, population control and on and on.

"People today believe these lies. What we have to do is get back to common sense principles. It's going to be an uphill battle, but it's something that we have to do. God raised the Tea Party for this reason—this change has got to come from the grass roots. The people at the top are the ones bringing the problems. They are the select elite who actually believe it's their responsibility to rule and to control the mind and thinking of other people.

"If we're going to save our country, it's going to take more than talking to just our kids about these principles. We're going to have to take the offensive. We're going to have to take the battle to those who want to destroy our nation. That's what I believe with all my heart.

"Kids are in government schools. They're being trained to learn collectivism. They are not being trained to think through issues. Everything now is an 8-second sound bite. You are taught now how to learn, rather than how to think. That's backwards.

"What we're being taught, and what they want us to learn, are totally diametrically opposed to what we have learned as American citizens. Today, we're told that we have to put our national sovereignty aside in order to embrace globalism. This idea of globalism isn't something new. It started way back in the book of Genesis Chapter 11, when Nimrod and his followers decided to make a name for themselves by building a tower to Heaven.

> Then they said, "Come, let us build ourselves a city, with a tower that reaches to the heavens, so that we may make a name for ourselves and not be scattered over the face of the whole earth.'
> (Genesis Chapter 11, Verse 4, NIV)

"God said that, because they were of one accord, they'd get it done. So He said, 'We have to go down and confound their speech.' That's where we get that story of the Tower of Babel. That's where we get all these different languages now.

"The enemies of American citizenship are of one accord. They are generational. One group dies and another group picks-up the same mantel and keeps moving. They die off, and that's why concerned people, today, have got to stop looking at individual issues. These people are looking at cap and trade, sustainable development, population control, same sex marriage, animal rights. They're looking at all of these different issues as separate entities, and picking which ones they want to harp on, rather than realize it's a satanic agenda that involves all of these things.

"People who are talking about globalization want controlled elections, a controlled media, controlled education, elimination of free speech, disarmament of the population through gun control, and bogus fiat money, which is nothing but funny money. They want a national healthcare system, global government, and on and on.

"We have to realize that we have a battle on our hands here. It's a battle of freedom versus slavery. It's much more than us trying to educate our kids on American principles. We've got to deconstruct the lie that's put in their heads from post-modern globalist thinking. After we deconstruct that lie, then we've got to reconstruct what they were supposed to learn.

"My wife teaches in public school. We don't even call it "public school" anymore; they're government schools set up with an agenda to get the kids to learn socialism and globalization, rather than Americanism.

"I graduated from high school in 1961 and when I was in school, we were taught civics. We had prayer in the schools. The year after that, they took the prayer out. They took out the Bible reading. They took out the 10 Commandments. They took out 'Civics.' They took out 'Phonics.'

"There is a reason for all of this stuff. The agenda now is well-entrenched as a stronghold. It's a spiritual battle. The reason parents don't know this is because they haven't been trained to recognize it. This mess has been going on since Genesis Chapter 11.

"I saw the switch in American policy and American thinking in the 60s because I came of age in the 1960's. I began to see America turning a corner to the left, the far left.

"I'm looking at this and, yes, I was under Jim Crow segregation at the time but even under Jim Crow segregation, I still knew America was the best country on Planet Earth. I always had pride in America. America was my country. I never thought about giving up my American citizenship to move to Haiti or move to Africa or move to communist China. It's ridiculous.

"God put me in America for such a time as this. I've always loved our country, even with our blemishes and our race problems. Now, years later, I'm looking back and seeing that we're fighting forces from Hell.

"These are spiritual forces to destroy America. Why? Because God raises up America to a 'city set on a hill.' God raised up America according to the Psalm of David when he said "Blessed is the nation whose God is the Lord."

"Now, we've put the Lord aside, and we'll believe in every other kind of mess. We don't want to hear anything about the Lord. Now we're being cursed because conversely, if we're blessed because we obey the Lord, and we're now cursed because we have forgotten the Lord.

"We've got to do a whole re-education process, first deconstructing the spiritual and moral lie, and then reconstructing it with solid biblical truth and Constitutional truth, which is based on Americanism, constitutional principles and American sovereignty.

"It's going to be an up-hill battle, but people are beginning to wake up. That's what the Tea Party movement came from. The opposition has not figured out how to stop the Tea Party. They wish they could figure it out, but they can't figure out how to do it, because there's no "leader" of the Tea Party.

"The Tea Party cannot be co-opted because it's not a political party. It's people who are saying, 'Enough is enough. Something is wrong here in America.' Most of the people in the Tea Party are older people, people in their 40s, 50s and 60s. Why? Because they have seen this paradigm shift in America, from the way America was to the way America is now.

"People come up to me and say Americans want this and Americans want that. And my question to them is always this: 'What Americans are you talking about?' Evidently, half of Americans want socialism and communism and globalism and believe in same-sex marriage and believe in abortion and believe in population control, so what Americans are you talking about?

"Are you talking about Americans who love America? Or are you talking about Americans who are American in name only? They're citizens of America, yet in their hearts, they're not loyal to America and they're working to destroy America, and to bring a one-world government, a one-world economy, and a one-world religion in order to fulfill the Bible prophecy that was written thousands of years ago regarding the rise of the Anti-Christ.

"This is what people don't understand because people have no spiritual understanding. They're living in spiritual darkness. The Bible tells them what all of this one-world government business and globalization and one-world economy and one-world religion is leading to, but they did not see it. The Bible has told us that, but we don't want to listen. That's why we're in the mess we're in."

Reverend Craft fears for the future of our children, because of the secularism that has permeated society, suppressing our faith and ignoring foundational principles, in addition to what they are being taught in schools.

"Students are being taught socialism. They're being taught globalization. They're being taught communism. They're being taught cultural correctness. They're being taught political correctness.

"They're going to lose their freedoms and their ability to govern themselves and live according to the ways of God. So, the question is, what's more important? The deficit, jobs and taxes, or our children being Americans?

"You have so many Americans, especially young Americans who do not know how to think. They don't think through the issues. They hear something come out of Washington in an 8-second sound bite and they believe that. They don't think through it and say 'Is this really so? Let me examine that before I come to a conclusion.'

"They're coming from a post-modern mindset, where everything now is no longer black and white; everything now is grey. Grey is the color of deception, because it's a mixture of black AND white, truth and falsehood. Once you start dealing in areas of grey or post-modern thinking, then anything is permissible."

Craft and his wife have raised good kids, but he isn't sure what they might tell you about America beyond that it is a great country. Asked what his kids would say about being American, here is his response:

"To be honest with you, I have no idea.

"All of our children have college degrees. They're all doing well. We've raised them all with a love of this country, for the most part, even though we weren't cognizant of it or specifically set out to do that. For us, in our generation, it was just common sense.

"All of my kids were born in a different generation, after 1960. They all have been programmed to think "globally"—that's just a fact of life. At the same time, they realize that they are in the most blessed country in the world, and the things they've accomplished, they couldn't do anywhere else.

"What I can say, speaking on their behalf, since they're all grown with children themselves, is that without a doubt, they think this is the greatest country in the world. I don't see any of them relinquishing their American citizenship. That I can say without a shadow of a doubt."

Craft has some thoughts on what parents can do to undo the information their children are getting everyday from the media and the education system, that he believes promotes one-world governing and diminishes American sovereignty.

"The kids are thinking about being global citizens, about America just being a small piece in the village. We have to undo that thinking in our kids, especially if they're grown, to get them to see that that's wrong. That's leading down a path that they're really not going to want to go down. But they don't know that, because that's all they've been taught.

"If you have kids in government schools, you have to undo the nonsense they put in your kids' heads every night. They're not learning— learning has been exorcised out of the schools. The left is censoring the truth of American citizenship and American sovereignty. It has been replaced with global thinking, moving toward a one-world government.

"We have to take the idea of censorship and turn it back on them. We've got to say, 'You guys accused the religious right and conservatives of censorship but why have you censored the textbooks? Why have you taken out the religious writings of the founding fathers? Why, when you are elected into office, do you put your hand on that Bible and swear to uphold and defend the United States Constitution? The moment you put your hand on that Bible, you're lying, because you have no intention of keeping that promise because you think the Constitution is out-dated and has to be revised as a living, breathing document.'

"This has been going on since Genesis Chapter 11, and we are going to have to go on the offensive and say, 'Okay, you people oppose censorship. Then why have you censored textbooks? Why have you taken out American principles and replaced them with global thinking? Why have you exorcised all that the Founding Fathers said from the textbooks, so that our children in government schools today have no idea about their heritage? Why have you done that? If you are opposed to censorship, then put the original source documents back in there instead of taking them out.

"We're in an ideological and spiritual war. The stakes are eternal, therefore this is no kind of war you're going to play with kid gloves on. You're going to have to get fighters who are going to go into the enemy's camp and fight.

"Jesus said we are to be salt and light and when we lose our saltiness, we are nothing and we're trampled under the feet of men. That's exactly what's happening in America today.

"We have been sitting back too long, and letting the liberals take the offense. Now we're trying to put out fires that have become an inferno. We're losing our nation. We're losing our country."

★ ★ ★ *Key Points* ★ ★ ★

- We must preserve America's sovereignty by fighting against the notion of globalism.

- Remind your children that America is the best place on Earth.

- God wants us to be independent nations, not one world government, according to the Book of Genesis.

- Teach your children to think, not just learn things.

- We are in a fight against what has become the new norm. We must stand up for ourselves and our nation for our children's sake.

Chapter 4

CHARACTER

Jackie Gingrich Cushman

★ ★ ★ ★ ★

Jackie Gingrich Cushman is a syndicated columnist for Creators Syndicate, author of *The Essential American—25 Documents and Speeches Every American Should Own*, speaker, wife and mother of two children. She is also the daughter of the former Speaker of the House, Newt Gingrich.

Her unique perspective, having grown up around her father's political activities, is due to an avid in interest government and history. Here she talks about how she was raised, and how patriotism was instilled in her.

"I was born in New Orleans, but my sister and I were raised during our formative years in a small town in Georgia—Carrolton, Georgia. My father was an assistant college professor and my mother was a high school math teacher. It was a small town, which was great for growing up.

"My father started running for Congress in 1974, when I was 7 years old, so I had a little different experience, because that's my memory of growing up: being part of the congressional campaigns, being involved with fairs, Fourth of July parades and Memorial Day picnics, and all the things that a rural, Southern district would do in the '70s, if you can imagine that. Those activities formed the foundation of my upbringing. Never were we anywhere where we didn't think about country and patriotism and God and the importance of those who came before us and what we could do to make our country better.

"Even though Dad lost twice, he won that third time. Many people thought he was crazy, running that third time. What that experience instilled in me was 'persistence matters,' which is a great lesson to teach children.

"Serving the country and pursuing what you think is right for the country, sometimes takes a lot of personal toil and effort, but, in the end, if that's what you think is right for the country, then that's your duty -- to pursue what is right.

"If you can imagine the 1970s in a rural Southern district: at that time, the offices of the 6th District of Georgia were located in South Fulton, which meant the southern part of Atlanta, which really meant the poor side of Atlanta. The district extended all the way down to Griffin, Georgia, and all the way west to the Alabama border.

"It was a huge geographic area, obviously pre-Internet and pre-computer. The only TV station was in Atlanta, which we would never really use for advertising because it was too expensive and didn't cover the territory. So you were basically left with a drive to every place, a crossroads stop at the rural gas station and grocery store, shake the hand of two people who were there, and move on.

"We spent a lot of time on the road as a family because we all went wherever Mom and Dad went. There were no nannies in our home. My grandmother, my mom's mom, did help out for quite a while but we were on the road a lot with them.

"We folded and handed out flyers, stuffed and stamped envelopes, and handed out and put on bumper stickers on cars. You name it, we did it! And that's just the way it was. It was our life! We had a lot of fun. Losing twice made us realize winning was a lot more fun. Losing may build character, but it's not necessarily fun especially when it's three in the morning."

Cushman speaks about what historical figures and documents really influenced her own patriotism and how she uses these to teach her children.

"You really have to look at Abraham Lincoln. Obviously he was a great president and a great man, but would not have had the fortitude to do what he did had he not had those losses early on. I think people forget that. They forget he went through a 'Wilderness Period,' when things were hard, but that's part of what made him the great president that he was.

"There's a really good biography out called *A. Lincoln: A Biography* by Ronald C. White. It's an incredible biography that takes you through Lincoln's writings and speeches, and how they transition through his public life. It's really interesting.

"I have a nine-year-old son and an 11-year-old daughter. Part of what we try to do in our family is build character. The other night, my son and I were talking about something. He was having a hard time, and I said 'Stick with it honey, it's going to get better.' And he said 'Mommy, I know and if it wasn't hard now, I couldn't prove later that I had improved.' And so he gets it.

"My point is this, as families, we tell stories. We tell stories in my family about my dad losing and then winning, so we talk about persistence. We tell stories about my mother's mother, who left the farm, against her father's wishes, with the egg money her mother had saved to move to Columbus, Georgia, and become a nurse. She was the first child to go away and get something above a high school education. She obviously valued education.

"As a nation, to build this national character, we have to very deliberately and very purposefully tell national stories that reinforce the character traits that we want our children and all people to have.

"Let me give you some very specific examples. I just finished researching my book called *The Essential American*. In this book, I have compiled, edited and created an introduction for 25 documents and speeches that I think every American should own and read. To me, they're essential. They include Patrick Henry's 'Liberty or Death' speech, the Declaration of Independence, and The Constitution. We have Theodore Roosevelt in there. We have Abigail Adams. We have lots of Lincoln, obviously, Franklin Roosevelt, John F. Kennedy, and Martin Luther King.

"Part of what we are trying to show in my book is that those types of positive messages not only portrayed the trials they went through, for instance the American Revolutionary War, but also show how we came out as a nation and what made us able to do that. For instance, belief in God. If you look at the Declaration of Independence, clearly we're a nation that believes in God. We believe God gave us rights and that we loan those rights to the government. That is very different from any other nation on the earth.

"It's important that we talk about *that* American story and *that* American transition to our children, so that we can instill these values in them. A lot of what we do has to be done through re-telling American stories and explaining to our children why they are so important.

"There's so much noise and so much frantic activity, especially at election time. I've already taught my children that they should not believe everything they read or hear on TV because most of it is not true. I learned that the hard way. When I was in grammar school, I read things in the paper about my father that were factually incorrect. Since then, I've known everything you read, you take with a grain of salt. Just because it is in the newspaper does not mean it is true.

"You have to think about it—is this actually real? We are in this cycle of negative advertising and talking about how terrible things are in America and how awful it is and how people are terrible. It's kind of like having a family where a parent berates a child unmercifully for errors committed, but forgets to tell the child that he is actually a wonderful person. Think about how that would demoralize a child. He would no longer *want* to be good because he's been told repeatedly that he is terrible. What's the point in trying to be good?

"I tell my kids stories about my dad winning. I tell them stories about how I was told that I would never be a syndicated columnist, and now I am because I worked hard for years to get there. I tell them stories that transmit the values I think are important for them to know.

"We need to be very careful as a culture, about saying things like 'people are always going to throw mud and say terrible things.' To transmit the desired values and culture, it is important to focus on the core values we want to reestablish in our communities. Let's tell stories about those values and make that the focus of our efforts.

"Terrible things do happen, but let's talk about the good stuff. Let's talk about Abraham Lincoln saving the Union. Let's talk about how he had the Emancipation Proclamation in his pocket and didn't pull it out until he got a sign from God, which was the Battle of Antietam. Let's talk about how the plans of the South leaked out and the Union Army learned of the plans, and that's how they won. Let's talk about those good stories.

"There were times in the Civil War that if Abraham Lincoln did not have the fortitude that he had, things could have been very different. Clearly, we could have had a different future, a much smaller, much less bright future. But he stuck with it.

"I really do believe in reading the documents and speeches. I spent a month reading and loved it. It really reminds us that, from George Washington through Lincoln through FDR and even JFK and Bush's 9/11 speech, there is always this underlying belief in God as a higher power. We're here because of Him. We have rights from Him.

"That provides a lot of the ability to weather, to persevere, and to keep going. We need to remember that. That's part of our concern today. In today's secular society, perseverance has been sacrificed and not supported. That's a tragedy, and we need to correct this with our children."

Cushman talks to her children a lot. They don't watch much TV because they are reading and discussing. Here she talks about how this has made a difference in what her kids would tell you if asked why they love this great country they live in.

"They'd say 'We love freedom.'

"We're an interesting family. We don't watch a lot of TV. We don't have it on during the week at all. Just today, I had a parent/teacher conference for the kids. One of the things the teacher said was, 'It's really interesting. For most students, I have to tell the parents to make sure and talk about current events, because their child doesn't seem to be aware of what's going on in the world. Yours is one of the two in the class who has this knowledge.'

"I said, 'That's funny, because we don't watch TV.' And she said, 'No, but you talk about it.' We talk about current events when we have family dinners. We sit down and we talk to each other. That's part of how we teach them.

"My son loves history, and he loves the military and military history. He knows about all of the major wars. The other day in class, the teacher brought up the Bay of Pigs and he said 'Oh yes, wasn't that with Fidel Castro and Cuba?' He knows we broke away from the British because they were trying to tax us without representation. He understands that when our voice is heard, we stand for freedom. He would be able to articulate that pretty well, as would my daughter.

"You can express this in daily discussions involving your children. Part of the challenge is making the time as a family to sit down together. So much information can be shared over the family dinner table. And include children in the conversation, so they're not just listening but also contributing to the dialog.

"Sometimes that means the conversation might be a little slower, a little different than you might like, but we have found this to be really effective. People would be amazed at how young children will understand concepts we assume they will not understand. They have a much greater grasp of things than most people realize.

"Also we give the kids allowance. The children have certain chores they have to do to earn it. Occasionally, they *don't* earn all of their allowance. Whatever they earn of their allowance is what they have to use for giving to the church on Sunday and buying all of their toys and candy. My husband and I don't buy any of that for the children anymore. We just started allowances last year when my youngest was 8—that seemed to be the age when it would work. The child needs to be old enough to understand but young enough to not want anything that's too expensive.

"My son saved money for four weeks to get a certain item that he wanted. My daughter saved her money for what she wanted. I've watched them make these financial decisions. My daughter sometimes turns to me and says 'That's just not worth that money.' You have to create these artificial constraints so they *have* to make the decisions. That's how people learn, when they actually have to go through the process themselves. We've had a really successful time with that.

Cushman's favorite way of teaching her kids about our most important documents and concepts is from stories, either from books, from living the experiences at famous locations, or by simply telling them stories she has learned.

"We have a lot of kid's books we've gone through with them. We have also gone to Washington, DC, a couple of times, because we could actually walk through the buildings and see the original source documents. We went to Boston and got to see where the Boston Tea Party was. We also did the Freedom Walk. We tell them stories. I think all people, whether they are children or adults, like stories, stories like Patrick Henry's 'Give me liberty or give me death' speech.

"My son had grabbed a hold of the Theodore Roosevelt story. Roosevelt was born a sickly, asthmatic child who couldn't do much, but he decided to work hard. He was an outdoorsman and a "Western" kind of guy. He talked about the strenuous life. His whole story is about perseverance and fitness and vigor and getting involved. He could have retired to a family estate and done nothing with his life. He chose not to do that. The real American heroes reflect the values we want to pass on to our children."

Cushman tells a great story about the way her son expressed his understanding of patriotism.

"We had just returned from the parent/teacher conferences. My son had written about a friend of ours, who is now an American citizen, but who had emigrated from Cuba after his father was shot by Raul Castro. He fled to Europe for a few years before he was able to come to the United States. He worked very hard and became a professional violinist.

He became first chair for the National Symphony Orchestra for the violin and just recently retired.

"Meeting people like him and hearing his story, emphasizes why America is different; it is because we are actually free. My son experienced that same understanding. He got it. He understood why our friend came here and why that friend loves this country and why America is different than Cuba.

"Part of exposing them and explaining the differences that make America great is so that they, in turn, can turn around and tell those stories, continuing to share that information with others. They have not only heard it, but they understood it, and they understand the differences. That's the next level of learning—when you get it and can repeat it to someone."

Cushman talks about how important God was in the founding of this country and how it cannot be ignored. The founding of our country was based on principles we received from God. Teaching this to our children is imperative.

"When you look at the Declaration of Independence, it says we declare ourselves free, and we're created by God. We are a nation of people who believe in God. You can look at Abraham Lincoln's life. He was incredibly faithful and became more faithful during the war, as did George Washington. Washington, at one point, had several horses shot out from under him and bullets shot through his clothes. Truly, at that point if you were him, you'd think, 'There has got to be a reason I'm here. There has to be a greater purpose in my life.' These are the stories that should be told.

"Faith, perseverance, hard-working risk-takers. If you look at the people who came across the ocean because they were fleeing religious persecution, they took a huge risk. There was nothing. No Ritz-Carlton, no Four Seasons. And when they came over here, they had to make sure they had everyone and everything they needed because that was it! You needed to have a guy that could make shoes, and a person that could do this and a person that could do that. Talk about taking a risk!

"We are historically a nation of HUGE risk-takers. Unfortunately, if you become too comfortable personally, you don't like to take risks. You have a lot to lose. Sometimes, we need to remind ourselves it is ok to take risks, and you have to be able to take risks in order to make huge advances.

"If you have a faithful people who persevere, work hard, are risk-takers who believe that God gave them their rights, which they lend to the government, that is a great set up."

Finally, Cushman feels strongly that there is a very big difference between being called 'American' and being called a 'patriot.' Here she illustrates the distinction between the two.

"Technically, you're a citizen of the United States if you were born in this country. Unfortunately, not everyone born here understands what it is like to be an American. They are technically American, but then you look at someone like our friend I mentioned, who emigrated from Cuba, fleeing a totalitarian regime, who became a citizen and loves America like few people I know. He loves America, can't say enough about America. He's a true patriot.

"A patriot is someone who truly understands why our system is different, truly understands how we got here, and truly understands that he or she actually has a role to play in our country. We're not here just to sit back and let things happen for us.

"To be an active patriot and citizen, you have to actually be involved with the country. That's the real difference. If everyone that was born here could have the understanding of what America really is, then there would be opportunity for everyone to really understand how incredible our country is and become a patriot.

"We have so many freedoms. We have so many opportunities. We are so different than anywhere else in the world. The challenge we have is to teach those who are born here how incredible our country really is."

★ ★ ★ *Key Points* ★ ★ ★

- Tell stories to your kids—make history interesting. By reading the original source documents together, you can instill a love for this country and illustrate the struggles and risks our Founders took so that we could have what we have today.

- Discussions with your children may take longer than with an adult but remember how effective it is for a child to think through ideas on their own.

- Teach your children about perseverance and character. Even though it might not be easy to do something, sticking to it definitely has its rewards.

- Discuss current events as a way to stay aware and to teach them how to question if something sounds right or not in the media.

- Consider giving your kids allowance as a way to teach them the value of money and about how to make their own decisions about things they want.

- Visit historic places as a family.

- Patriots don't have to be born in America to be true patriots.

- God must be recognized as the cornerstone of our country's founding.

Chapter 5

FAITH

Erick Erickson

Erick Erickson is the editor of Redstate.com, the author of *Red State Uprising: How to Take Back America*, a radio host and a CNN contributor. He is married and is the father of two children.

Erickson had a fascinating childhood, having spent a good chunk of his formative years outside of the United States. This absence actually kindled his love of this country. Unlike the vast majority of Americans, he *has* lived in a country where he had to hide his religion and respect the local culture so vastly different than his own.

"My parents were both registered Democrats who were from conservative families. Well, my mother's family at least. My father's father was actually a union activist and an FDR guy. He had come to the country right at the turn of the century. He blamed Herbert Hoover for all of our ills, but hated the United Nations, of all things.

"I'm somewhat unique in that I grew up in Dubai, United Arab Emirates. My dad worked for Conoco Oil. When I was 5 years old, we moved there in 1980 and returned to the US in 1990 when I was 15. We were there during the Iran/Iraq war. At the time, everyone just knew that there was some guy named Ronald Reagan who was keeping us safe.

"When you shipped things overseas, you shipped items you would need by air cargo, which got there quickly. The rest went by ship, which got there six months later. All of my books were accidently put on the ship. So, my bedtime stories at night were from the only available reading material in the house -- William F. Buckley from *National Review*. I was indoctrinated at an early age.

"The central component of our lives was that, even though we were in an Islamic country, my parents insisted we go to church. We would have to sneak off in the middle of Sunday night—Sunday was a work day, not a weekend, to a local school and meet with other Christians, discreetly carrying our Bibles as we went.

"We would come home to the states for a couple of months in the summer, generally for the Fourth of July. But overseas, it was a very different thing. There were no Memorial Day celebrations, no Veteran's Day celebrations, nothing like that.

"My dad worked offshore for seven days, and then was home for seven days. We lived in a typical subdivision, no walls around it, right out in the middle of the city. We went to an American school just down the street with other Americans and many other people from around the world."

While they had to be discreet with their Bibles and the practice of their religion, faith remained an important part of Erickson's life. Here he talks about the parallels between faith and the founding of our country.

"To be a patriot, you have to have some component of faith. The quintessential core belief of American patriotism, the cornerstone, is the belief that we were destined to be the 'shining city on the hill.' You've got to have a faith component to really believe that.

"I had lunch with Dick Cheney right before he left the vice president's house. He, at the time, was reading *1864: Lincoln at the Gates of History* by Charles Bracelen Flood. It's a fascinating biography, I have since read, that really goes from January 1, 1864 to December 31, 1864. I've never read a biography that covers only one year.

"*The Weekly Standard*'s Executive Editor Fred Barnes was also at that lunch, and he asked Vice President Cheney if he believed that there was some divine hand in American destiny. The Vice President didn't really answer the question directly, but said, 'You can't read that book and think that everything that happened in that year was coincidence.'

"People forget that four weeks before the election in 1864, the Union was in disarray, devastated. People were rioting in the streets. Then all of a sudden, Sherman took Atlanta. Grant had wiped out Lee's army. And then there was the election."

For Erick, American history in middle school in Dubai was a very different experience than it was once he got back to the states, where he took an additional American history class in high school. He talks about the difference between American history taught in an American school abroad and what he learned here in the United States. The differences are striking and helped formed his opinions early on.

Erickson points to the fact that teaching about the founding of our country is largely missing in many schools today. The focus is on the special groups within our country, as opposed to the foundation upon which everything else lies.

"In Dubai, we studied American History in 8th grade. We were required to read the Constitution line by line in order to understand what a profound document it was. We had to read the Declaration of Independence too. We learned about the struggles of the American Founders, like Sam Adams and his family, and the struggles and the destitute situations of the men who pledged their lives, fortune and sacred honor to the Declaration of Independence. We learned about the struggles of the generals in the Civil War, such as General Lee's torn allegiance to Virginia versus the United States, and General Grant who had to fight against people with whom he went to West Point.

"The struggles we learned about were different struggles. They were the struggles of the people who were leading the country versus the people who were being led.

"In contrast, 11th Grade American History focused on the struggles of the American Indians, the struggles of the slaves, and the struggles of the Civil Rights movement.

"It makes a profound difference when you see what the people who were leading the country were going through. They were losing their children. They were losing their homes. Yet, they continued the struggle for a cause they believed in, a cause greater than themselves.

"You ask someone today what they know about the Connecticut Compromise of 1787 also known as the Great Compromise of 1787 and their eyes glaze over.[2] But how very necessary that was as were the

2   The Connecticut Compromise or Great Compromise came during the Constitutional Convention and became the basis for the way the legislative branch of our government was originally structured. It gave the states proportional representation in the House of Representatives based on population and structured the Senate so all states are equally represented. Senators were originally elected from within each state's House of Representatives by the members of the House, not the general population. The American public did not elect

Virginia and Kentucky Resolutions, written by Thomas Jefferson and James Madison.[3] These struggles were essential in the founding struggles of the founders of our country. But people don't pay attention to these struggles anymore. They are much more interested in the Civil Rights Era, which *is* important but you can't understand the Civil Rights Era unless you understand the struggles of the founders of our country.

"The interesting thing was that my 8th Grade American History teacher in Dubai was a profound liberal. I was in 8th Grade in 1988 during the Dukakis/Bush election. We did mock debates, studied that presidential election, and questioned why the election was structured the way it was. The Constitution has the answers. It tied everything back to the original documents. *The Federalist Papers* were mandatory reading in 8th Grade.

"This is an educational component that is often missed. People just aren't interested in teaching the history of this country. They are more interested in teaching the history of certain groups within the country."

Although Erickson's children are still young, he has already started talking to them about our country, and why things are the way they are.

"I'm the political one in the family, and I try not to talk politics with my children. My wife, on the other hand, has been explaining to my daughter why she goes to private school and not public school, or the 'government school' as they refer to it together.

"My daughter has started asking questions already, like 'Why are there 50 stars on the flag?' and 'Who is the president?' and things like

United States senators until 1913, when the 17th Amendment was passed, allowing for this to happen. (source: pg. 113 *A Patriot's History of the United States* by Larry Schweikart and Michael Allen and The Constitution from The Cato Institute)

3 Written by James Madison and Thomas Jefferson in 1798 and 1799, respectively, the Virginia and Kentucky Resolutions attempted to revive the Anti-Federalist sentiment calling for state sovereignty and trying to draw a distinction between the citizens of the states and the states themselves. The resolutions attempted to determine the power the states have as they relate to the federal government. No other states supported these resolutions for fear that, if they were upheld, many states would succeed from the Union if they disagreed with federal laws. The counties would succeed from the states, and then towns would succeed from counties. (source: pg. 152 *A Patriot's History of the United States* by Larry Schweikart and Michael Allen)

that. She asks these questions and we try to answer. For example, the Fourth of July this year, we talked about why people explode fireworks and what the celebration is really about.

"She has memorized the Pledge of Allegiance and the first few lines of *The Star-Spangled Banner* in school and what they were talking about in order to understand the struggle those people went through in order to build our country. There are some parts she doesn't understand, but she understands there was a great fight. And there was a king, and we didn't want a king anymore. We wanted to govern ourselves but to do that, we had to be responsible."

Asked about what else beyond faith really helps form patriots, Erickson points out that understanding history is vital for our children to understand and appreciate being a patriot.

"I do think there is a huge faith component, but there's more than that. You've got to understand and appreciate the actual history of the country, what a Puritan work ethic is and where that term comes from. Faith is the starting point, but you've got to understand the fight. You've got to understand what The Revolution was all about. You've got to know your honest history.

"Our five year old had been getting picked on at school. My wife told her, 'You're only a victim if you choose to be.' Think about the Founders—they chose not to be victims. It seems like most people today would rather be victims and get sympathy. It's disturbing how many people are willing to go that route. People have no appreciation of what the founders went through.

"One of my 5-year-olds first questions was asking me to explain who the people are on the money, to explain who that guy is on the penny and why he was worth being there and the guy on the quarter and the dime and the nickel. It was a great jumping off point to introduce Abraham Lincoln, Franklin Roosevelt, George Washington and Thomas Jefferson."[4]

★ ★ ★ *Key Points* ★ ★ ★

- Teach children to appreciate the freedoms they have in this country as compared to other countries.

- Understand that faith was an underlying component of our country's founding.

- Focus on the Founding Fathers and our early history, not the history of the special groups.

- It is never too early to start talking about our country and its history. Talk about the flag, our presidents, and our freedoms. Talk about why certain people are on the money as an introduction to your children about the presidents.

---

4 According to page 32 in *The American Patriot's Almanac* by William J. Bennett and John T. E. Cribb, Franklin Roosevelt is on the dime because of his advocacy for the establishment of the National Foundation for Infantile Paralysis, which is now known as The March of Dimes. The organization was founded in order to help wipe out polio, a disease from which President Roosevelt himself suffered. His image began appearing on the dime in January 1946 following his death. Before that, females representing Liberty appeared on the dime.

Chapter 6

ACTION

Cathy Gillespie

★ ★ ★ ★ ★

Cathy Gillespie is a co-founder of Constituting America with actress/activist Janine Turner. She is a long-time political strategist and philanthropic activist, including serving as the Chief of Staff for United States Congressman Joe Barton of Texas and the director of W Stands for Women as part of the Bush-Cheney 2004 campaign. She is married to former Republican National Committee Chair Ed Gillespie. They have three children.

Their son is a college sophomore. Their older daughter is a high school senior and their youngest daughter is a high school freshman. Their younger daughter is in her first year of boarding school—a choice she made. When her daughter decided to go to boarding school, Cathy knew she had to make sure her daughter was ready in the sense she would know about the founding principles once she got there since Gillespie and her husband wouldn't be there to talk about these things with her each night.

"She really begged us and researched all these schools online and has ended up at Saint Andrews in Middletown, Delaware. In trying to make sure she was well grounded before she went off to boarding school, I was almost desperately going over the founding principles of our country and the Founding Fathers with her. It's a great school, but I felt this extra sense of urgency to make sure I had instilled in my daughter everything that I felt she needed to know before she left.

"What's really cool is that in her history class, they're actually using a lot of primary documents. They did a debate and used *The Federalist Papers* as a source. She ended up using our website, ConstitutingAmerica. org, and some of the essays that our guest constitutional scholars had done on *The Federalist Papers* as a reference. So, that was kind of neat."

Gillespie and her husband have a rich American heritage that really illustrates the greatness of the American people and the opportunities this country affords its citizens. This heritage and her ancestors' hard work really influenced Gillespie in her own love of this country.

"My grandmother used to talk to me a lot about what a great country we have. She came from a very poor family of migrant farm workers, who went from farm to farm picking cotton. They didn't have a home. She was probably born in 1907, so this was around 1920 or so. They had a covered wagon that they kept all their possessions in, and if they were lucky when they were working a farm, there would be a little shack that they could stay in while they were working there.

"She would always talk to me about how, in this country, if we work hard, we can do anything. And even though she couldn't graduate from high school because her family needed her to work, she still ended up being a business owner and owning several houses as investments, renting them out to people. She always talked about opportunity and hard work, and that is really what this country stands for. She even managed to send my mom to college.

"My grandfather was in World War II. I remember going over to my grandparents' house, and we'd sit down, and my grandmother would show me pictures of him during the war. He was involved with the construction side of things. A carpenter by trade, he was never involved in a battle during the war. He was stationed by the Panama Canal, and then in Alaska for a time, working on air strips and an Air Force base. My mom and grandmother went to Alaska and lived there for a time to be near him.

"My grandmother would tell me about the war. She was always so proud that her husband had served, and that she and my mom went and lived on base around the soldiers. That's really where some of my very first fundamental beliefs came from: loving this country, appreciating the freedoms that we have and the opportunities available to its citizens.

"We go back to the Revolutionary War on my side of the family. My mom is a member of the Daughters of the American Revolution, and my dad is a member of the Sons of the American Revolution. They've spent a lot of time tracing their ancestors.

"My husband's father has a really neat story. He came to America when he was about eight or nine years old. He was one of five kids that came over with his mom. They traveled from Ireland on a cattle boat.

"Ed's grandfather, his dad's father, had been over here for a couple of years, working to earn the money for the rest of the family to come. Ed's dad had very vivid memories of going with his mom and his brothers and sisters, and getting on the boat and traveling over to the United States. He remembered what life was like in Ireland. He had such a great appreciation for the opportunities that came to him in America, because he basically came to this country with nothing but the clothes on his back.

"He had an 8th grade education. He served in World War II, and actually earned a Silver Star, two or three Purple Hearts, and a Bronze Star with an oak leaf cluster. He was a true war hero, and he wasn't even born in this country. He just had this fierce love of America, because he had lived somewhere else that did not have the same freedoms and opportunities, and so he knew firsthand how special the United States of America is."

During her childhood, Gillespie's parents involved her and her sister in many different activities that sparked an interest in government and our country in a very soft-pedal way—not overt, not forceful, but certainly enough to encourage and inspire Gillespie to want to make a difference in our country's history.

"My parents were never overly politically active, but they always voted and they would talk to us about how important it was to vote. We would talk about current events around the dinner table in the evening. They encouraged me to get active at an early age. I remember, during Watergate, I felt sorry for President Nixon. That must have been a sign of my future political party affiliation. I remember I wrote him a letter and told him that I was going to keep him in my prayers, and was thrilled when I received this little postcard back from the White House. That was a really big deal.

"Another time, I told my dad that I wanted to see a President in person. When I was in the 7th or 8th grade, President Ford came to Southern Methodist University to speak, and my dad took me to see him. We stood behind the rope line. I remember seeing the big limousine pull up, and President Ford got out and waved. I thought that was the greatest thing ever. I got to see a President! So even though my parents weren't really politically active or plugged into politics in any sort of big way at all, they always did what they could to foster, in my sister and me, an interest in government and what's going on in the world.

"Veterans Day and Memorial Day were important to my parents. After my grandfather passed away, especially on Memorial Day, we'd go out to the cemetery and put flowers on his grave. They instilled in me how important it is to honor our veterans and honor those who have fought for our freedoms. I do have early memories of going out and putting flowers on my grandfather's grave. Those are some of the things that I remember growing up."

Gillespie talks about how the fundamental principles of opportunity, service to country and true love of this country instilled in her from her parents, grandparents and her husband's family influence how they've raised their own children.

"I have always talked to them about my grandmother. I have a picture with her and her brothers and sisters in front of the covered wagon they took with them that contained all their possessions. We would also spend a lot of time with Ed's dad telling stories about when he was a little boy in Ireland and all kinds of family lore, because Mr. Gillespie, being Irish, was a great storyteller.

"The themes of his stories were always the value of hard work, and opportunity. He would tell our kids about all the different jobs he had when he was a young boy, trying to help his family make ends meet when they had just come over from Ireland. Mr. Gillespie, just like my grandmother, ended up being a business owner. He owned several businesses and was one of the most respected men in the community. He achieved all of that because of the freedom and the opportunities that our country offers to those who want to take advantage of it.

"We have a replica of a poster that was on some of the boats that traveled over from Ireland to the United States. It's called 'Advice to Irish Immigrants' and it says:

'In the United States, labor is there the first condition of life, and industry is the lot of all men. Wealth is not idolized, but there's no degradation connected with labor. On the contrary, it's honorable and held in general estimation. In the remote parts of America an industrious youth may follow any occupation without being looked down upon or sustain loss of character, and he may rationally expect to raise himself in the world by his labor. In America, a man's success must altogether rest with himself. It will depend on his industry, sobriety, diligence, and virtue, and if he does not succeed, in nine cases out of 10, the cause of failure is to be found in the deficiencies of his own character.'

"We have this hanging on our wall in our family room, because this is our family's philosophy. It was instilled in Ed by his dad.

"It's very important for kids to understand their roots. They need to understand the founding roots of our country. They need to understand the principles on which our country was founded, and the sacrifices that people have made through the generations in order for us to have the freedoms we have. But they need to understand their family's roots as well, and how their own family has embodied those founding principles. That's what we've tried to do with our kids. We always remind them of where they came from, and what the lives of their grandparents and their great-grandparents were like. We also talk about the American philosophy. These stories show our kids where they fit in, in our country's history. For example, when they were studying World War II, we talked about what their grandfather and their great-grandfather did in the war. It's so important that kids know their grandparents' and their great-grandparents' stories."

According to Gillespie, knowing your family's history and retelling those stories to your children is so important. It is a very important way parents can teach their kids about the core values of this country, and about being good citizens and patriots. She also has other ideas to help educate your children.

"Another really important thing to do is to take your kids to historic sites and talk about the history of our country as they see these places. If you happen to live on the East Coast, you can take advantage of the historical monuments, the Civil War battlefields and Revolutionary War sites. This is a very valuable way to teach the history and core values of the country.

"And it's important to read with your kids, historical fiction and historical nonfiction as well. Some of the best memories I have are reading the *Dear America* books with my daughters.[5] There's a great one on the Revolutionary War that got them very interested in that period of the country's history. It's historical fiction based in fact.

"Dinner table conversations are also so important. I remember a time we had talked quite a bit about the founding principles of our country, of freedom, of economic freedom, of how important it is to not over-regulate business. When the healthcare bill came along, I knew that I had taught my daughter well when she proactively said to me, with no prompting, 'Mom, don't you think the Founding Fathers would just be rolling over in their graves if they heard about this?'

"Of course, exposing them to the primary documents, the Constitution, the Declaration of Independence, even *The Federalist Papers*, is also very important. When we were doing a study of *The Federalist Papers* for Constituting America, my youngest got pretty interested in it, and even wrote an essay about the Electoral College that was very insightful.

"It's important that these kids learn to delve into the primary documents, because they are not often looked at in school. If we're

5 These books are available at www.scholastic.com and profile four fictitious girls, each from different periods in time – 1620, 1777, 1912 and 1941. They are written by various authors.

going to make sure our kids get exposed to them, it's going to have to be done in the home.

"The thing about kids is that they love any sort of ritual or repetitive act that you participate in. Something as simple as just reading from a book every night becomes a really special time they look forward to. These little rituals are not just fun, they are comforting to them.

"Another thing parents can do is to encourage their kids to enter our contest, the "Constituting America We the People 9*17" contest, where they talk about what the Constitution means to them and how it is relevant today. The younger kids can draw artwork or create a poem. Even if they're not entering our contest, have them create things to express what their country means to them. It's one thing to feed a child information, but it's another to let the child take what they've learned, synthesize it, come up with a project on their own, and actually create something. It is then that they truly internalize what they have learned.

"My daughter was so intrigued by her grandfather's story of coming from Ireland that she wrote a little book about it when she was in fourth grade. It wasn't a long book. It had dialogue and filled in details that she imagined. She included his interaction with his brothers and sisters, how he felt on the boat, and how he felt when he first saw the Statue of Liberty. The book covered his whole life. Now, anytime we need to know anything about Ed's dad's life, we always ask her. She's the expert, because she wrote this whole little book about it."

Gillespie asked her older daughter what she loves most about this country. Here is her answer, along with different views all of her children have of the world, different from our generation and our parents' generation.

"I asked my daughter what she loves most about our country, and she said it's the freedoms we have that other countries don't have. She actually has a young man in her U.S. government class this year, who moved here from another country. He talks a lot about the differences between the countries. All the kids' eyes have been opened to how different life is where he comes from compared to life in our country. Likewise, he can't believe some of the freedoms that exist in our country. He is continually amazed by it. He's always saying things like, 'You're kidding' or 'You can do that here?' It's been a great experience for all the kids. My daughter has become very cognizant of the fact that our country has many freedoms that other countries do not.

"The other thing our kids feel is very important is the equal opportunity afforded all people, and the fact that equal opportunity didn't always exist. My daughters get very indignant when we talk about the time in our country when women didn't have the right to vote. We talk about segregation, and we talk about the civil rights struggle. In their generation, they have seen so much more equal opportunity than ever existed in previous generations, and that's something that they value and they think is very important.

"A recurring theme that I hear from my kids is the fact that they've grown up knowing that anything they want to do is possible, because of the freedoms and opportunities we have in our country."

Gillespie's children are in a position not every child will be in during childhood, but the things they have been able to do *because* of their parents' involvement in politics is sticking with them and they are influencing other kids their ages.

"They've been exposed to some things that a lot of people aren't exposed to. They've gotten to spend time at Camp David and be with the President, in sort of an informal setting, and Secretary Rice, and listen to discussions about world affairs. Not anything top secret. My son has been to two Republican National Conventions. They probably understand a little bit more than most kids about how government works and the political process, and they have an appreciation for how hard our elected officials work. They have a respect for people who sacrifice in service to our country.

"When you actually know elected officials, rather than just read about them in the paper, the fact is most people who serve, whether they're Republican or Democrat, make an extraordinary sacrifice. They work very, very hard, and most of them don't earn as much money as they could if they were working in the private sector. They don't get to see their families a lot. My kids have an appreciation of the efforts made by all people who serve our country in that way.

"My youngest has been involved in student government. She ran for student body president and was elected. Our family's campaign experience probably helped her in that, because we were always talking to her about, 'You've got to make sure--have you counted your votes?' and 'You've got to turn your vote out and make sure everybody comes to school on election day,'"

Gillespie summarizes what parents can do to really help instill patriotism and love of country in their children with some specific action items and fundamental principles.

"The most significant thing parents should do when raising their kids as good patriots is try to boil down the founding principles of our country: limited government, personal responsibility, individual freedom and economic opportunity. If our kids are not grounded in those principles, they might be more easily swayed by anything that comes along, whatever the latest 'cool' trend is.

"When they actually understand the principles on which this country was created, and look at the incredible progress we have achieved over the past nearly two and a half centuries, as compared to any other country on Earth, and look at the fact that our Constitution is the oldest constitution still in use in the world, then they know not only what they believe, but why they believe it.

"We are sort of this 'American Idol' culture now. Things go in and out of popularity so quickly these days. Something's cool one minute and not cool the next. It's important that kids internalize these eternal founding values so that when the world is going by really fast, they can judge what they're seeing based on these principles and values.

"The most important value that we can teach our kids is to be engaged, active citizens finding ways to make a difference in their country. If they see a problem, work to do something about it and don't look the other way. It starts with voting, and that's why it is so important to take your kids with you to vote so that they can see what that's all about at an early age. My son was so excited to vote in the '08 Presidential election, and he's been a good consistent voter since then.

"Encourage your children to volunteer in their community. My son went to a work camp through our church, and my daughter participated in a program with her school where a few kids went to Haiti and to volunteer over Thanksgiving. She was actually there about a month before the earthquake, and she's still been really involved with helping Haiti in many different ways ever since.

"We can teach kids the values, and that's important, but we also have to teach them to translate those values into action so they can actually make a difference."

★ ★ ★ *Key Points* ★ ★ ★

- Tell stories of your family history and the country's history to help them see the value of hard work, perseverance and internal fortitude.

- Honor our veterans on Veteran's Day and Memorial Day.

- Take your child to see the President if he (or she) visits your area.

- Listen to what your children say to you and their friends about how they feel about our country and important issues and discuss these things with them.

- Have your children take action—vote, volunteer, start something that doesn't already exist, let them see the amazing opportunities taking the initiative can offer a child.

- Visit historical places.

- Talk to your children about how the United States allows for equal opportunity that other places don't.

- Read historical fiction and non-fiction with your children.

- Visit historic sites as a family.

- Discuss how serving our country as a public servant is a very difficult and yet, rewarding job.

- Talk to your children at the dinner table about our founding principles.

Chapter 7
DUTY
Rick Green

Former Texas State Representative Rick Green is a speaker for Wallbuilders, a Texas-based organization focused on family and promoting faith and morality in our culture. Wallbuilders also has one of the largest collections in the country of original documents from early American history. Green is also an attorney, president of the Torch of Freedom Foundation, an author and a radio host. He is married to Kara and they have four children.

Here he speaks about his childhood and how it influenced him to become a strong patriot and pass that along to his children.

"More than anybody, my dad was constantly pumping in my mind knowledge of the country's history, where we came from, and how blessed we are as a nation. He passed that torch of patriotism to me. Throughout my education, I was fortunate to have teachers, including my mom, who loved our country and reiterated the greatest aspects of America. They didn't spend all their time talking about our mistakes, but actually talked about America being exceptional and what made us special.

"I was blessed in that regard. As soon as I was on a college campus, I got involved politically and started holding rallies for the troops. This was during Desert Storm in 1991. There was something about bringing people together for the cause of supporting those troops, and supporting our nation, that just gave me the bug. After that, I just had a real passion for honoring the sacrifice of those who were willing to lay down their lives for us, not just by giving speeches or clapping for them at events, but by *living* our freedom. There's so much we can do to honor their sacrifice. That hit me at a young age, and ever since then that's what we've devoted our time and energy to."

Green talks about why he felt so inspired to make a difference by holding rallies and supporting the troops, even at the young age of 19 years old. What he found from these rallies was how much impact his effort could have on people, and how much of a difference people *can* make when they put themselves out there and take a stand.

"I had a lot of friends that were over in Desert Storm fighting. Some of us were just sitting around saying, 'What can we do?' We had been watching television and seeing anti-war demonstrations. None of us are *for* war, but these were really anti-troop rallies. They were even holding the flag upside down. We were 18 or 19 years old, sitting around wondering, 'How do we respond to that? What can we do here on our little campus out in our little school in west Texas?' We said, 'Well, if they can do that, then we can do a rally *for* the troops.'

"So we held a candlelight vigil on campus. I skipped a lot of classes to organize it, but we did promote it and organize it, and hundreds of people were there on this little campus. After I spoke, we talked about why we were having the vigil. A mom of one of the troops came up crying, saying, 'Thank you,' because we read all the names of all of our friends who were over there fighting. Something about seeing the mom's appreciation, made us realize the extent of this sacrifice. I'll never forget it. It is like it was yesterday. It really impressed upon me that you can impact lives if you're willing to get involved. If you're willing to go out there and put yourself on the line and say what you believe and fight for the things that are right, it will make a difference.

"In this case, it was an expression of appreciation that made a difference. It wasn't changing a law or anything like that, which you can also do, but it still let me know that you *can* impact lives."

Green's children are part of his speaking tour now. They each have their own topic regarding the Constitution on which they speak. This involvement has a two-fold effect: it reinforces patriotism in the children and sets an example for other kids that it's good to be a young patriot, and it's ok to love your country.

"Our oldest is 14 years old and our youngest is 7 years old. They travel the country with us when I go out and speak. And they're an integral part of our program. They actually get up on stage and recite the Declaration of Independence.

"We started doing something new this year. We started teaching the Constitution more specifically. My 14-year-old now gets up and teaches the first amendment. He goes through the five freedoms, and talks about what they are and how to live them. Then my 11-year-old teaches the second amendment.

"They're getting more into the details. In the past, we've always done kind of the philosophy of those basic principles that were set up for the nation. And now people are hungry. They want to know more. It's really exciting, because the audiences at the places we go desire to know more, to dig deeper. This has allowed our kids to also go deeper and not only learn the information, but teach it as well. When you teach it, the learning is reinforced.

"It also gives the children a chance to share the information with others, and not just memorize it. It's one thing to learn by rote memorization. It's another thing to understand what you have learned and how it impacts your life."

At his speeches and at the mock Congress he helps run in the summers, Green is discovering that more and more parents are making an effort to teach their kids about being a patriot.

"I really believe that there are an awful lot of parents that are doing the same thing, because I get to work with these young people that are a little bit older than my kids, 16 to 25, at our Patriot Academy that we conduct. It's a mock legislative session. The kids spend a week with me at the Capitol here in Texas. I'm telling you, these kids are amazing. They have a stronger foundation and are much more grounded in the principles and in what makes our nation great. And they're passionate. They're articulate. And that doesn't happen by accident. That tells me that more and more parents are raising American patriots. The more parents that do this, the more likely we are to save our country. It's even more important, now, for we the people to make sure that we are encouraging and inspiring and sharing great stories of great American patriots throughout our history, to try to raise up a generation that will say, 'America's best days are not behind us.'

"American exceptionalism is not based on what moment in time we happen to live in. It's based on principles that are timeless and it's about bringing those principles back to the forefront, getting our schools to teach it, and encouraging parents to teach it.

"When you put the principles in place, they flat out work. We're the most successful nation in history for a reason. It did not happen by accident. I would much rather encourage parents to teach that to their kids too."

Green helps conduct mock Congresses that brings our governmental process to life for young adults. Here he talks about how this really helps children better understand politics and government, and inspires leadership and involvement in the future.

"We had 22 states represented last summer. They come from all over the country. We literally take over the Capital. The reason we do it here in Texas is because I used to be a legislator here, so we have access. They are on the real floor of the House. They're in real committee rooms all week long. We designed it to be exactly like a real legislative session, so they learn the process. At the same time during that process, we're teaching the Founding Fathers' philosophies and views. They learn skills, everything from speaking skills, to media skills, to how to work a room. These are some of the most basic skills they learn in order to successfully go into business or politics or journalism, whatever they're going to pursue. We just want them to be good leaders, leaders with integrity. Just go sit in the gallery of the Texas Capitol the first week of August and listen to these young people. You'll be so encouraged. I tell you, the help is on the way."

Green's children are a bit unique in that they speak about patriotism and loving their country all the time. Here he speaks about what he believes they feel about their country and what they would tell someone if asked why they love their country.

"They want their lives to mean something. They want to know that they've had an impact. I can already see that in my 11 and 14-year-old children. For example, my 14-year-old is already talking about wanting to go into the military and serve. There's definitely this sense of responsibility and an understanding that freedom is not free. He will not be a leech on society that just enjoys the benefits, but never gets involved in preserving it for the next generation.

"My children have a sense of duty and responsibility. They've already been in 43 states. They've seen the battlefields. They've seen the museums. They have visited all those sites. And you just can't take all that in and *not* have an appreciation for what we have.

"Our family created a book called *Our American Story*. It's about our travels and my time in the Legislature. We show the kids visiting all these sites. We challenge people to raise patriots. We say, 'Plan your vacations, not around a beach or other entertainment, but around historical sites. You can still have fun; you can ski or you can go to the beach or whatever, and at the same time visit an historical site that your kids will never forget. There's nothing like going to those historical sites and actually seeing them.' Make it fun. Don't go do the boring typical tour thing. Come up with some great stories to tell your kids as you are driving and bring history to life. They're going to remember."

The Green children can't help but be interested in the founding documents, based on what their dad does all year long. Here he tells a little bit about how they got involved in his presentations.

"We really stumbled into it. When my oldest boy was about 6 or 7 years old, he started going with me when I would fly out for a speaking trip. He started picking up on some of what I was doing. We started just having fun with it, like memorizing the signers of the Declaration of Independence. After we memorized all 56, then I started telling him stories about some of these guys. I guess he heard me speak enough that he heard me recite the Declaration, because I always use the 56 words out of the heart of the Declaration that they recite. So he memorized it and asked, 'Well, can I try it?' He was little, about 7 years old. He started doing the 56 words during my presentations. The younger ones started seeing him doing it, and they wanted to do it too. As he got older, he passed the baton to the others. Then, I would teach him something new that he could start presenting."

In speaking with your own children, Green has some thoughts about what we can do to inspire the interest and desire in our children to learn more about their county and its founding. He admits his family is a little unique, since that is part of their daily lives, but simply telling the stories to your children will peak their interest.

"Just take the stories of the founders and start teaching them to people. I'm a big believer in telling the stories. I think children get bored only learning dates and places. Tell stories about historical places and people. That's how God does it in the Bible, keeping it interesting. I think that's the way we should teach history. I hated history when I was growing up. I had no interest in it. David Barton, from WallBuilders, is the person who got me interested in history, and made me start enjoying it, because of the way he tells the stories.

"That's what our family tries to do; teach through stories. We also have lot of books that are stories about great Americans. By having the children read the stories, or by reading to them, they get to live that life a little bit. To me, that's the best way to instill in them an appreciation for history, encouraging them to want to be somebody who makes a difference."

Besides exposing your child to fascinating stories in our history, Green says parents should also help their children apply these principles and ideas to their own lives, so they can fully appreciate the freedoms they enjoy as Americans.

"Just looking for life situations where you can say, 'Well, aren't you glad we have this right guaranteed in the Constitution that keeps that from happening to us?'

"It's no different than teaching your kids about faith. You look for those life circumstances where you have a teaching moment. I believe you can do the same thing with history and the founding principles. Look for examples. I always take one of my kids in to vote with me. Even when they're 7 years old, and they get to push the button, we talk about what that means and why getting to choose the person you vote for, rather than having your leaders forced upon you, is special. Getting to actually participate in these activities seers the experience into their minds.

"One of the best indications of a child's learning is what they say about what they have learned. I'm starting to see a lot more of that with my older son. I'm seeing his buddies start to talk about what they're going to do, where they're going to go to college, what they're going to do with their lives. I am thrilled to hear them talk about sacrifice and being willing to serve our country first *before* whatever else it is that they want to do.

"My kids have definitely had some fun, anecdotal stories about bringing up topics regarding the Founding Fathers and that sort of thing, but I think my younger ones are in the memorization part of learning. It's always fun when they get things confused. We have a good time with it."

Green shares a funny story about his oldest son during Rick's first session in the Texas House of Representatives. His son got some hands-on experience, both during the campaign and during Rick's session.

"My son was 2 years old during the campaign. Everywhere he went, he was the star of my campaign. He was on the commercials saying, 'Go vote my daddy.' It was great. He would come on the House floor with me during that first term and sit by me. It was kind of fun.

"In the Texas House, they ring the bell for a vote. You have 150 people there so there's a lot going on. It's a little bit chaotic; people are having conversations and not necessarily paying attention to a particular vote at that time. The ones that are for an issue start walking around holding up a number '1' trying to indicate to the people that they know are with them on that particular issue, vote 'yes,' even if you weren't paying attention. Or they hold up a number '2' if they're against it. You see all these people walking around holding up 1s and 2s. Well, Trey was 2 ½ years old, and he's walking up and down the aisle holding up a '2' all the time. So, the Speaker said, 'Yeah, he's a Republican - voting "no" on everything.'

"We had our second and third children during my second session, but they were too young and never really got to do anything at the Capitol. And then our fourth came along after my term was finished.

"This last year, in the primary, I ran for Texas Supreme Court so I had a statewide campaign. We put a wrap on our bus and the family went on the road. I thought they would just be worn-out and hating it by the end of our travels. Well, I ended up winning the primary - got first place out of six, and then I lost the run-off, just barely. We were out of it in April.

"As fall got closer and closer, my oldest boy wanted to campaign again. My state senate seat was supposed to open up. He was pushing harder than anybody else to try to get me to run again, because he just loved the campaign and being out there on the campaign trail. I was glad, because I was afraid I was going to burn them out on it."

Green talks about what words he would use to describe the most important value being a patriot teaches our children.

"The first word that came to mind for me was 'duty,' because I think that's what's missing in our culture. We don't instill a sense of 'You do your duty, regardless of the results.' It's like voting. You vote whether your candidate wins or not. You don't give up and go home and say, 'I'm not going to do it anymore.'

"When you teach patriotism, there's a sense of responsibility to others first, before self. That's what gets across to them when you teach God, country, service, those kinds of things. They develop a sense of duty that says, 'It's bigger than me. So, if I don't do it, I'm actually hurting the greater cause. I need to do it whether I get the results that I want or not.' Whether it's running for office and you don't win, or you support somebody and that person doesn't win, or you work for a piece of legislation and it doesn't get through, that doesn't change the reason why you go out and do your duty. The founders were very focused on knowing your duty, doing your duty and shouldering the responsibility of duty. Hopefully, that is what your children will walk away with if you teach them about patriotism."

The final principle Green speaks about is faith, the role God played in the founding of this country, and how important it is for our children to learn this, too. He also talks about how we must vigorously defend this presence of God, and not allow it to be removed from our country's philosophical foundation.

"For us, that's certainly at the top of the list of what we teach. The founders would have said the same thing. That's why the Declaration talks so much about a Creator. Jefferson mentions Him four times in the document, emphasizing the fact that we are endowed by our Creator.

"God-given rights cannot be taken away. If your rights are dictated by your neighbor or from government, they can easily be taken away. That element is essential. A lot of my friends will say, 'Well, you can teach patriotism without God. You can just teach the principles of freedom and responsibility.' And I have to remind them of what George Washington said, that religion and morality are indispensable supports of political prosperity. He said, 'Of all the habits and dispositions which lead to political prosperity, those are the most important.' He also said, 'In vain would that man claim the tribute of patriotism who would subvert these great pillars.'

"When we talk about raising patriots, we have to leave the 'God' piece of it in. If that piece is removed, then it's all about what can I get for myself or what can I take from others. There's no parameter. There's no boundary on the freedom. When you recognize that God is the source of your freedom, there is a boundary. There is recognition that if I'm going to live my life enjoying this freedom, I have to live it respecting the authority of the source which gave me that freedom.

"I love speaking at Tea Party events and consider myself one of them, but there's definitely a small element in the Tea Party movement of the more libertarian mindset that wants to leave God out of it and only talk freedom. They don't realize where that road goes. It just will not work. It leads to chaos. It leads to tyranny every time without God in the equation.

"When we talk about raising patriots, that quote from Washington is essential. I'm not saying everybody has to be a Christian or anything like that. But there has to be recognition of a Creator, recognition that His power is the source of all freedom.

"My boss, David Barton, talks about it all the time. You've got to be on the offense, not just the defense. We sit back and wait all the time, trying to defend the ground that we haven't given up yet, when, in fact, we need to go on the offense, trying to take back some of the ground that we've lost over the last few decades. That's really the shift I've seen in our movement and in the mentality of freedom-loving Americans is; they are no longer sitting back. They are saying, 'We're going on offense and we want to gain ground. We don't want to just defend ground.'"

★ ★ ★ *Key Points* ★ ★ ★

- Teach your children about our founding principles and founding fathers, and let them repeat what they have learned so you can hear how they grasped a concept. Rote memorization won't stick with them. Tell stories to make it interesting.

- Talk about the country's history and the blessings of freedom your children reap today because of that history.

- Be a role model as our duty as citizens. We must vote and stand up for what we believe in, regardless of the outcome. It's the principle that counts, but be strategic in your choices.

- Plan vacations around historical places.

- Encourage your children to attend mock Congress camps and seminars to learn how government operates.

- Don't let God be taken out of the equation. The presence of a greater power than us is essential in understanding our nation and its destiny. Stand up for that—defend it to show your kids how to stand up for their beliefs.

- Encourage your children to rally their friends and take action even if it is not the "popular" idea—encourage them to stand up for their values.

- Encourage them to defend the greatness of this country and actively promote it. Be proud to be American.

Chapter 8

HISTORY

Kevin Jackson

Kevin Jackson is a nationally-known speaker, consultant, political pundit, and author of *The BIG Black Lie –How I Learned the Truth about the Democrat Party*.[6] He also contributes to several websites including Andrew Breitbart's Big Government, American Thinker and Townhall.[7] He lives in Saint Louis and is the father of four boys.

Jackson was raised by his grandparents after the death of his mother when he was just 5 years old. He remembers asking them, after listening to a speech from Ronald Reagan, "Why are we Democrats when what we believe is what that guy just said?" He tells his story of the influences that brought him to love this country and become a conservative.

---

6 Amazon best-seller
7 Big Government (www.biggovernment.com), American Thinker (www.americanthinker.com) and Townhall (www.townhall.com)

"My grandparents were Democrats. It wasn't a love of country that they instilled. It was a feeling that there was nothing I couldn't do.

"My influences were from Hollywood back then, to be honest with you. I really tried to tap into it when considering how I became "me," and watching old war movies and just feeling like 'America has to win!' How Hollywood depicted America then as opposed to now when we get our butts kicked and everybody's like, 'It was a great movie; America got its butt kicked!' I grew up watching the John Wayne movies; that certainly was one influence.

"The idea those movies presented was you can be anything you want, you can do whatever you want and tying that together with our military and our great country. I connected the dots myself, because it's not like we flew flags on the Fourth of July, and my grandparents walked around always talking about how great the country was. They never talked *down* about the country.

"If they talked down about anything it was usually about Republicans, but they didn't talk down about them. It was more like, 'Democrats are good; they're for the people." But I never ever felt like Republicans were bad. It was more like "Democrats are good, so we're not Republicans." Now, I never believed that. I knew we were Republicans.

"I always had this feeling of being a fighter and fighting for our country. I remember the body count that the press would always report during for the Vietnam War. They would put up '45,000 VietCong were killed today. 3 Americans were killed,' and I remember thinking to myself 'Holy Cow! How come we haven't killed every Vietnamese known to man?' I just remember as a kid going 'Yeah, look at that.' It was us versus them. And if we were at war, doggone it, we were supposed to win it! So all of that tied together created my opinions."

Jackson has four boys. He talks about how he has raised them to be patriots by thinking for themselves, and he admits to having a strong influence over their political sway.

"They were doing the count in Florida for the Bush/Gore election in 2000. I remember I was watching TV in my bedroom with my oldest son who was ten at the time, as they made the map of Florida blue, which meant Gore was going to be president.

"I remember lamenting that there's no way Florida is going to go to Gore. My son was sadder than I was. All of a sudden Dan Rather says something like, 'There's been a change in Florida; Florida is going to go red, we are calling Florida for George Bush.'

"I'm not exaggerating - I jumped SO high, I touched the ceiling with my hands. And I'm not a tall guy! I almost leaped through the ceiling literally, and my ceiling was easily 10 feet high. My kid and I were high-fiving each other. So my kids grew up very Republican and conservative. Then my oldest worked on the Obama campaign during his freshman year in college, which of course, perplexed me. But what are you going to do? You say, 'look, he's a young kid.'

"Now what's interesting about it is he didn't do it because he was such a huge Obama fan; he did it because he was learning the dynamics of politics and the real world. His college acquaintances were geeked over Obama, and he wanted to be part of the enthusiasm. It was more of a sociology experiment. He later informed me, 'I'm not a Democrat.' However, he was also distrustful of Republicans too. So he's still one of my apples.

"Unlike me, my oldest son wants to be a politician. He'll probably end up running on a Republican ticket. He's going to Harvard after he gets out of Wharton. My other kids are conservative, and I don't think any of them will get caught up in anything close to Obama hoopla, when the next election occurs. When you talk to them about conservatism, they get it.

"The apple doesn't fall far from the tree, but certainly they are their own people - thinkers, for sure. None are just drones of their father, though there are times I might prefer they were."

Jackson talks about why parents must help break the cycle of misinformation. Just like superstitions we learn as kids, the information our kids learn often sticks with them. As parents, we really must get in front of so many things in life for them. Otherwise, they form their own opinions based on the information they are getting from the media, from friends and other outlets.

"Be proactive," Jackson says.

"A lot of kids these days get told something and they believe it forever. You tell them if they walk under a ladder, it is bad luck, you have people avoiding ladders. Think about it; why would walking under a ladder give a person bad luck? But if a parent (or somebody a person trusts) says this to a child at an early age, you will watch 50 year old men afraid to walk under ladders.

"You know the saying 'step on a crack, break your mother's back?' When I was a kid, I wouldn't step on a crack. Now, as an adult, I don't consciously think about it, but I found myself avoiding cracks on sidewalks, as ridiculous as that sounds. But it does prove my point that there was something in my psyche that associates 'stepping on a crack' with bad luck because I learned that as a kid. I found myself avoiding these inane superstitions that I remember as a child. If a black cat ran in front of my car, I'd be parked for 2 days![8]

"All these superstitions. I remember declaring one of my fears out loud to one of my friends and catching myself and thinking, 'How stupid is that?' So you hear something and there's nobody to correct

8 Not true, but Jackson admitted to having turned around to avoid that stretch of road.

you. For example, with my youngest son I say 'Oh the boogeyman's going to get you!' and I'm wrestling with him, and then I stop wrestling with him and I'll say, 'You know there's no boogeyman, right?' and he says, 'I know.' I don't want him to be afraid of the boogeyman, because the boogeyman doesn't exist. To teach kids to love a country, you've got to tell them how to do it so they will remember and correct anything they have learned that's not true.

"I tell my kids the reason why I go shake that old man's hand is because we have our freedoms because that man protected our freedoms. And when you see a veteran, you should be very proud, and you should go up and thank them.

"You teach them. You ingrain these thoughts of honor. You tell them they are privileged to live here."

Our founding documents are the backbone of this country. Kevin spoke about what he thinks about these documents, the founding fathers and how, even today, race is still part of the discussion.

"The Constitution is an interesting document, particularly along with the Declaration of Independence. The argument? Is it a living breathing document, or is it a stoic document that is full of principles by guys who were out of touch with what's going on today?

"My explanation, for quite a long time, has been that the Constitution was written by men who were flawed but who had incredible insight too. Fifty-six founders, 12 of whom owned slaves, even though the majority of them gave their slaves away, or tried to. (You couldn't give away slaves easily back them.)

"With respect to the fugitive slave laws in the Constitution, you can see that the framers of this document had set it up so slavery had nowhere to go but to end. That's the only way to interpret it. When they wrote it, it would have been so easy to write that 'all men are created equal, except our slaves.'

"The people who argue with me and say, 'Look at the provisions in there for slavery,' are not constitutional scholars. If they studied the Constitution, they would understand that the Founding Fathers were actually writing out slavery. They understood man's inhumanity to man through slavery and they knew to mandate the repeal of slavery with the whole population would be grossly unpopular since slavery was 'in' at the time. The Constitution was written in such a way that forced the end of slavery. They wrote it in such a way that it did everything it was supposed to do and it put checks and balances in place that allowed the people to always rule.

"What's interesting about the Constitution to me is that it shows you that race issues have ALWAYS been involved in the political discourse. And you would think that after 200+ years, we would no longer be discussing race. Do we talk about a woman's right to vote anymore? No. But we're still talking about slavery. We don't really talk about gender issues as they relate to politics except 'Who likes Sarah Palin and who doesn't? Who likes Hilary Clinton and who doesn't?'

"Race issues have been around for a long time and have affected our history. Race issues were the reason for the Civil War. Race issues cropped up again during The Depression and Reconstruction, because whites didn't want blacks to vote. They came up again during the time of The New Deal because of all the social programs attached to it. Race issues were central to the 1960s with the Civil Rights Movement. And even today, after the election of a black president, we are still talking about it. It's been in the fabric of America's socio-political discussion for a long time. I find it fascinating that it just doesn't go away."

Asked about what parents must teach their kids about being a patriot and loving our country, Jackson felt very strongly about teaching our kids about real history, not just the history they were taught in schools, which many times have a political agenda themselves. In particular, he believes many historical minority figures are not discussed because of this political agenda and that does not serve those kids well to develop pride in their country.

"Knowing your history—that's number one. People have distorted history. The only times blacks are recognized is during Black History Month—which I think is a ludicrous idea to begin with because black history happens every day! That history has been edited down to blacks were slaves and then they were freed and then there was the civil rights movement and they were freed again. Kids don't really learn anything.

"Here's an example of black history you don't hear about. I don't know if it's folklore or not. Supposedly, there was this kid, Jocko Graves. He was a young kid who stood on the shore and held the lantern so George Washington could see where to land the boat when he crossed the Delaware River. That crossing was significant because Washington was initiating a sneak attack on the British at what became the Battle of Trenton, a turning point in the Revolutionary War. This little boy was so dedicated, he froze to death in the freezing rain on Christmas for his country. He inspired what is now called the 'lawn jockey,' which actually originated from a statue George Washington commissioned as a tribute to this young patriot.

"So even if Jocko wasn't real, that's still a good story for a kid to know. If you were a young black kid, and you thought 'that's what we did to help in the war effort to save this country,' wouldn't that give you a bit of pride?

"To put it in perspective, we all know the story of the Alamo when everyone died fighting. They named the Bowie knife after Jim Bowie because he killed the Mexican guy who came to kill him. All of that is a farce. Davy Crockett and the rest of those guys tried to surrender, and the Mexicans killed them. But you have to have pride in Texas. Those men went down fighting, to the last man, even the sick guy who had a gun under his cover. When the Mexicans came to kill him, he killed one.

"They'll teach you about Davey Crockett and Jim Bowie, embellishing to no end to give kids a positive outlook, but they won't teach black kids about Jocko? What about Hispanic kids? I've often said if you took the average white person and you asked them for three Hispanics of historical record, that you learned about in history, and you would probably be able to come up with Pancho Villa and Cesar Chavez, you'd have to kill the son of a gun because he couldn't name you the third one.

"If you're not teaching the kids that the Mexican people have a proud heritage in America, then it's time to teach them that, otherwise, you're going to get kids hanging the Mexican flag in East L.A., because they have some source of pride in Mexico but not their own country."

★ ★ ★ *Key Points* ★ ★ ★

- Have pride in your country and be proactive in showing this pride.

- Remember how much influence you can have on your children and how they think about things. When you shake a veteran's hand and say "thank you," you are illustrating to your kids what respect and honor look like.

- Learn the REAL history, especially of the historical figures who were minorities, so all American kids can be proud of their county.

- Dig deeper and teach your kids to think for themselves so they can make their own decisions.

Chapter 9

COURAGE

Debbie Lee

★ ★ ★ ★ ★

Debbie Lee is a Gold Star mom and the founder and president of America's Mighty Warriors. She is also a spokesperson for Move America Forward, the largest grassroots organization that supports the troops in the United States, as well as for the Tea Party Express. She is the mother of two sons, and a daughter. One of her sons, Marc Alan Lee, was the first Navy SEAL to be killed in action in Iraq in August 2006.

As a Gold Star mom, Debbie raised what many would consider to be the ultimate patriot—a son who gave his life in the line of duty to keep others safe and free. Her story of how her son fought and ultimately died is something most of us cannot fathom, but illustrates true patriotism.

Her faith in God sustains her when most would falter. Her perspective on her son's fate, and her journey since, is truly inspiring.

In our interview, Debbie talked about how she came to love this country through her own means, having a strong military influence through her family.

"I had a pretty tough upbringing—very unusual circumstances. My mother got pregnant with me at 17. The circumstances were such that she didn't marry my father. My grandmother arranged for my mom, who was 17, to marry my grandmother's boyfriend so I wouldn't be born out of wedlock. Growing up, I didn't know that that wasn't my father. They divorced when I was 11.

"I went through some very turbulent teen years. My mom was going through the divorce and dealing with some other things that had happened earlier in her life. She went into the party scene so I left home when I was 16.

"I don't feel like there was anything particularly patriotic taught to me. I grew up in the '50s and '60s. We still said the Pledge of Allegiance at school.

"My high school years were right at the tail end of Vietnam. I remember turning on the TV and watching the nightly news and seeing or hearing the list of those killed in action or missing in action. I knew a couple people who had gone, but I had no clue what war was like. It's just like Americans today. They are so removed from war, unless they have someone who's in the military or they have a family member serving, they just don't get it. I would say the majority of Americans don't fully understand the sacrifices of these men and women.

"Looking back at my childhood, I know that one of the character qualities God instilled in me is 'Justice.' I want to see justice served whether it's terrorists attacking us or domestic issues. And I want to be there for those against whom injustice is being waged. I have always been the one who would stand up for the underdog.

"I've always known that my freedoms were paid for by those who served in our military. But to specifically go back through my childhood and say where that idea came from or when it was instilled, I don't remember. My mom's a little more on the reserved, introverted side and she never spoke about politics. That just wasn't done in our house. I know in high school I took some current events and political classes. I tended to be more on the liberal side back then and was even a card-carrying NOW member in my early 20s. But I think that was the rebellion in me."

Lee spoke about how she changed her mind later in life and now her faith in God led her to her choices. She also shares how she instilled that faith in her kids.

"I know where I stand politically has a lot to do with my faith. When I was 30, I completely gave my life to the Lord and surrendered everything.

"I've raised my kids to be very patriotic, to remember the sacrifices of our military men and women, but not to the extent that I am now. After losing Marc, 'freedom is not free' is not just a slogan; it is a reality. I understand that on a much deeper level now.

"All three of my children's lives were involved in the military. On 9/11, my oldest son, was serving in the Marines. My son-in-law was in the Army. Marc had just completed boot camp and my brother Jim was in the Air Force.

"It's one of those things—you see the handwriting on the wall. I knew I would have at least one family member who would deploy.

Lee also talked about her view on being a warrior, and how that characteristic is there from birth in some people. Her story of her son Marc's journey, and ultimate sacrifice as a patriot and a warrior, is very powerful.

"The warrior spirit is born in them. It's something that God develops in them. That's the way they come wired. I don't think you can make someone be a warrior; I don't think you can stop somebody from being a warrior if they're designed that way.

"I remember, during BUDs training, Marc got pneumonia and pulmonary edema and was 'rolled back.' He was hours from the point where he would have rolled forward and stayed with his class. He was rolled back and he had to start all over again in that class from the very beginning.

"At the same time, he fell in love with a gal who was anti-military, very liberal and convinced him, if he loved her and was going to marry her, that being in the military was not something that was conducive to family life. So he rang the bell and did what they call a 'Drop on Request' and since he still had his Navy commitment to complete, he was sent to the *USS Dwight D. Eisenhower* which was in dry dock in Virginia Beach. Because it was in dry dock, they assigned him to drive a shuttle bus on the Army base. I have a picture of him with his head on his arm on that big steering wheel, with a look that said, 'Oh, my gosh, what have I done?'

"I remember him calling and saying, 'Mom, what am I supposed to do? I know I made a huge mistake.' And I said, 'Marc, are you sure that's where God wants you?' and he said, 'Yes, Mom, I am.' I said, 'If you're not doing what God assigned you to do, you're going to come home and yell at your wife and kick the dog. Nobody is going to be happy.'

"Because of that conversation, and the searching in his mind, he put his packet in to go back to SEALs training. It took a year for him to jump through all the hoops because once you've rung the bell and quit, they don't look very fondly at bringing you back.

"People have said, 'Do you regret having that conversation with him?' And I said, 'No, he did what God designed him to do. He successfully completed his mission. And he's been redeployed to Heaven. I know where he's at.'

"On the day he gave his life, he stood up three times in a direct line of fire. It was 115°-120° over there. They had been in a fierce fire fight for about 2 hours. Marc carried the big gun so he was carrying anywhere from 150 to 180 pounds in addition to his own weight. I can't imagine combining all of those challenges and still be able to stay alert and physically able to continue on.

"Marc's buddy had been severely injured. The bullets had hit his weapon, and he had severe shrapnel injuries to his head. They could tell by looking at him, it didn't look good.

"Two of the SEALs dropped to their knees to help him. Marc made the choice to stand up in the direct line of fire to provide cover so they could get the medics up to the roof. The medic got up there and evaluated the situation and said 'We've got to get this soldier out of here immediately or there's no chance for survival.'

"So for a second time, Marc made that choice to stand up into heavy fire. Because he was designed that way as a warrior, he knew what he had to do. He didn't stop to weigh the pros and cons. He just knew it was the right thing to do.

"They all successfully got down off the roof and got the wounded soldier to safety. They went back to the base. The chief came in and said, 'We just found 30 of the insurgents who attacked us. Are you guys up for going back out?'

"I was in Camp Marc Lee my first trip to Iraq—I know that just on the other side of their base is a huge Marine base. If they had asked me,

I would have said, 'Go find some of those Marines who are fresh, who haven't been out in the last 24 hours.'

"That wasn't in my son's character. He looked at the chief and he said, 'Roger that. Let's go get 'em.' So they went back out and cleared several houses and went into the last house that Marc was to be in that day.

"They cleared the bottom of the house and started to go up the steps when Marc took the lead. As they went up, they drew fire through a window and, for one last and final time, Marc made the choice to stand in the line of fire to defend his buddies. He saved so many lives that day. I'm so proud of him and I miss him so much."

Lee's faith came to her rescue the day she learned of Marc's passing.

"I've been a widow for 16 years, so I'd walked through death before. But I can tell you losing your child is the deepest pain anyone can ever know.

"The night I got the call I was actually at my small Bible study group. My son called. There was nothing in his voice that alerted me. He said, 'Hey Mom, where are you?'

'At my Bible study, why?'

'Well, how long will it take you to get home?'

'I don't know—5 minutes? 7 Minutes? Why? What's up?'

"And he said 'You just need to come home.'

"When Marc left, I knew he wasn't coming home. I'm not a worrier; I'm not a fretter. Perhaps it was God trying to prepare me. I knew when I got that call, I knew what was waiting for me at home.

"As I drove home, I remembered a song from my past that says 'I put my hope in you, Oh Lord. Trusting You—I will not be shaken.

Knowing that you will see me through, I put my hope in you.' I just sang that song over and over and over.

"I got to the main intersection by my house, and there were probably 5 fire trucks and multiple police cars and ambulances blocking the intersection. I thought, 'My house blew up; that's all it is.' You think that's pretty bizarre to believe my house had blown up, inwardly knowing the other option that might lie ahead…

"I still don't remember how I got through that intersection but I got into my neighborhood and there were no emergency vehicles so I knew my house hadn't blown up. I expected to turn the corner to my house and see a black car parked out front, but as I turned the corner, there was no black car; there were no cars there.

"I saw my older son pacing on the sidewalk. I got out of the car and he said, 'Mom, the Navy's here.' And you know when you've got a child serving in the military, and the military shows up, it's not good news. I put my head on his shoulder and began to cry, 'No, no.'

"I walked in and because they had been trying to find me for a half an hour or 45 minutes, they had already been in my house for a while. They said, 'We can tell by looking at your home that you're a woman of faith. You're going to need your faith to get through what we're about to tell you. Your son Marc Alan Lee has been killed in action.'

"When my other son had called that night, I was at small group Bible study. We were actually celebrating my birthday, which had been the week before but we hadn't been together. My girlfriends gave me one of the Willow Tree® angels called 'Courage.' One girlfriend said, 'You just remind me of such a woman of courage.' I had no idea just how much courage I was going to need in the next half hour.

"My small group friends had followed me home. They came in and we just prayed and cried and talked about Marc and tried to process what had happened. After they all left, I knew where my strength would come from. God had been so important in my life and had proved Himself over and over. He promised to be a husband to the widow and a Father to the fatherless.

"My older son's wife was in Okinawa visiting her family, so he spent the night at my house. He went to bed and I went and grabbed my Bible. I knew from where my strength would come. I knew it would be difficult. I knew it would be probably the hardest thing I'd ever faced. But I knew God would give me the strength to get me through this situation.

"I opened my Bible to Psalm 27, Verse 1-3 and started reading:

'The Lord is my light and my salvation; Whom shall I fear?
'The Lord is the strength of my life; Of whom shall I be afraid?
'When the wicked come against me to eat up my flesh,
'My enemies and foes, They stumbled and fell.
'Though an army may encamp against me, My heart shall not fear.
'Though war may rise against me, In this I will be confident.'

"It was the perfect Psalm for that night. The second to last verse is 'I would have lost hope if I had not believed I would see the goodness of the Lord in the land of the living. Wait on the Lord. Be of good courage and he will strengthen your heart. Wait, I say, on the Lord.' I thought, 'Here is that courage again! There's a little theme God's weaving in here.'

"I have never audibly heard God but in my thoughts, he said 'I want you to read this at the funeral.' I thought, 'Are you kidding, Lord?' I just kind of paused and I thought, 'Ok, Lord, I'll walk through whatever door you ask me to walk through by your strength but it doesn't make any sense to me.'

"It's just amazing, some of the places that he has put me. I feel like, every morning in Heaven, there's a briefing and God and Marc get together and contemplate, 'Ok, where are we going to put Mom today? Whose life is she going to touch? Who's going to touch her life?'"

Lee is a warrior herself—even though she did not serve in the military, her journey with God, from her upbringing to the loss of her son, has brought her to a point where she does things she never dreamed of, and touches lives every day, teaching people the importance of loving this country and those who serve.

"The Warrior thing—God puts that in you. I believe all this hardship and the circumstances I went through as a child growing up built prepare me to endure what lies ahead. God equipped me with a personality that does not give up easily, to persevere.

"Whether God uses your parents or war movies, His hand is orchestrating your steps and directing you as to where you're going to be, your calling in life.

"Our nation is a nation founded UNDER GOD. That's where the patriotism also comes back in. We see the sacrifice that Christ made for us on the cross. Christ paid for our freedoms for eternity, and gave us freedom from the consequences of our sins. Our troops are willing to sacrifice their lives for the freedoms we enjoy in America. There isn't anything I wouldn't do for our troops, their families and the families of the fallen. I work 80-90 hours a week in service to our troops, their families, and those fighting for our country and our freedoms here."

Lee spoke about how parents can bring out the spirit of patriotism in their children by teaching them about the flag, its history, our country's history and about the sacrifice our troops are willing to make.

"It's important for parents to teach children these things. Teach them what the flag is, what the stars and stripes represent. Teach them the history of our country, the battles we've fought and won, how we established the freedoms that we have. Tell them stories of our patriots who have sacrificed and given so much.

"Whether it is World War I, World War II, or our Founding Fathers—instill in them that the freedoms that we have are not a coincidence. People have paid those prices for our freedoms.

"I homeschooled our kids so they heard a lot of those stories. We read about the Founding Fathers and what people sacrificed while establishing our country's foundation of freedom. Education is a huge part of being a patriot.

"Take children to patriotic events. Be there for the Fourth of July parades and don't just stand by the side of the road. Educate them as to why we celebrate on that day. Talk about the great country we live in. Instill in them the responsibility we have to vote. Talk to them about why it's so important to get Congressmen, Senators, and people in the White House who believe as our Founding Fathers did. That's what America is about.

"Many text books distort the truth in terms of history so we have to be creative to find our true history. Go to the library; find conservative website sites that give you recommended reading lists. Don't allow yourselves or your children to be brainwashed by mainstream media.

"As a teacher, I found that if you can use all five of your senses, no matter who you're communicating to, I can guarantee 100% they're going to get your message. So as we are teaching our children, we can speak to them, show them, do the hands-on experiences. Let them touch, taste, feel. Not just telling.

"And then hold them accountable to do something with what they've learned. That goes back to Marc's last letter home we have posted on the America's Mighty Warriors website—talking about those random acts of kindness. Maybe it's to babysit for a family whose father is deployed overseas, or take the family out to dinner or do something special at Christmas for a military family or send care packages to our troops.

"As a parent, you must act on what you're teaching your children. Be an example. When we are the leaders in our homes, we are an example. Children watch and observe. That's huge!"

Lee was a teacher and she homeschooled her children as well. She suggested using reenactment to help teach kids about the Constitution and other important concepts and documents. She also strongly supports seeing the actual historical places to help reinforce the learning for kids.

"Do a play of the events that led up to the signing or of when they were actually signing the Constitution. Any of those lessons where you can get more creative, where it's out of the box, it works a lot better.

"I would highly recommend taking your children to Washington, D.C. Go see Gettysburg. Go see The Capitol. I never was in Washington, D.C., until about 7 years ago. I was just *amazed* by what I saw. The paintings, the history. WOW! It's very impactful."

When Lee spoke about the most important concepts parents can instill in their children, it was the love of God, family and country which will produce the response of duty and voting.

"There is a duty and a responsibility that comes with freedom, that comes with being a patriot. Everyone may be required to give something different. Not everybody will be called to go out on the battlefield, but there is a duty and a responsibility, that come with the freedoms and the blessings we have in America.

★ ★ ★ *Key Points* ★ ★ ★

- The warrior spirit is born in some people and cannot be denied. Help foster that in your children.

- God helped in the founding of this country and gives us the faith to persevere. Make sure your children understand this intrinsically.

- Go to patriotic events such as Fourth of July parades and talk about why we celebrate our great country.

- Teach your children about the significance of our flag, about our history and about the stories of American patriots.

- Be creative in how you teach kids about the country—try to use the 5 senses to reinforce learning. Put on a play about the Founders.

- Stress to your kids that voting is a responsibility.

- Visit Washington, D.C.

- Challenge them to act on what they've learned about being a patriot such as babysitting for a military family, cook dinner for a military family or put together care packages for the troops.

- Remind your children that our freedom is not free.

Chapter 10

EDUCATION

Edwin Meese III

★ ★ ★ ★ ★

Ed Meese is the Ronald Reagan Distinguished Fellow in Public Policy and Chairman of the Center for Legal and Judicial Studies for the political think-tank The Heritage Foundation whose mission is "to formulate and promote the principles of free enterprise, limited government, individual freedom, traditional American values and a strong national defense," according to their website.

He served as the 75th Attorney General of The United States and was a senior member of the President's staff under President Ronald Reagan. He is also a retired Colonel in the Army Reserve. He and his wife have two grown children and five grandchildren.

His son is a Colonel in the United States Army, currently serving in Afghanistan. He is married and has three children, who are all three in college right now. His daughter is the mother of a nine-year-old and a five-year-old.

Meese talks about how he was raised during World War II and the influences both his parents and the military had on his upbringing. He also talks about how this military influence has affected his own children.

"I was born 1931. I was one of four brothers. My father and mother were always patriotic. They loved this country. My great grandfather, on my dad's side, had come over from Germany in 1850. He'd come across the plains in a covered wagon from St. Louis, Missouri, to San Francisco, California. My mother's side of the family came over from Germany.

"One of my greatest influences, with regard to patriotic thinking was, of course, growing up during World War II. I was 10 years old when World War II started. During the next five years, patriotism was a big thing in the United States. We were at war. People contributed to the war effort in every way they could.

"My father had been a soldier in World War I, just at the end of the war. He'd served six months before the war ended. He'd been a Private or Private First Class in the Army. When World War II came along, he was a little old for the Army. He was 45 at that time, and he enlisted as a volunteer in the Coast Guard Reserve. He spent several nights a week guarding the Port of Oakland and the ships in the port. He was also a leader in the American Legion, and was involved in a number of other civic activities.

"Patriotism was a part of the life of our family. My mother was active in civic activities, the Parent Teacher's Association and local civic organizations.

"Patriotism was just a part of our upbringing for my brothers and me. We were all in the Boy Scouts. It was not unusual for people at that time to be involved in various patriotic organizations even before the war.

"When I was growing up, patriotism was also an important part of what was taught in the schools. During World War II, there were radio programs each week that would talk about some phase of the war. That would then be part of your social studies courses in school. In grammar school, you learned a great deal about history and certainly even more in high school. Teachers were very patriotic and that was part of the curriculum. Saluting the flag was how the day began. So, that's kind of how we were raised.

"The books we read were an important part of this education. We got books from the library, which is perhaps a strange thing to talk about today. When I was a little kid, on Friday nights, our whole family would go to the library, where we would pick up books for the next week. In doing so, our folks would encourage us to get books that would talk about American history and similar topics.

"During World War II, there were all kinds of patriotic activities going on. There were patriotic band concerts in the middle of the city on Sundays. They had 'I Am an American Day' and 'Americanism Day' programs annually, and similar activities were a regular part of community life.

"Actually, patriotism and faith were heavily involved in my generation's upbringing. It was all part of the same kind of cultural assimilation, family background and education. To us, it was just a regular part of life.

"My uncle was in the Army, serving overseas during the war. The boy next door was in the Army. An association with the military was common and very natural for people in the community.

"I was in the Reserve Officers' Training Corps (ROTC) in high school. When I went to college, I received a letter in the fall of 1949, asking if I was interested in getting a reserve commission. I replied that I did. That is how I got into ROTC in college, which in turn led to a commission and, eventually, I went on active duty during the Korean War.

"After graduating college, I was actually in law school for a year before going on active duty in the Army. There were so many lieutenants pouring into the Army during the Korean War. Everyone was randomly assigned to a lot, and I was assigned to the 12th lot, which meant I didn't go on active duty for a year after I graduated. I was in the reserve in between.

"Eventually, my lot came up and I went into active duty for the Army, served two years, and went back to law school. I stayed in the Army Reserves for over 30 years after that. I was still in the Reserves while I was working in the White House, until I was appointed Attorney General. At that time, I had to retire, because you couldn't head a cabinet department and continue in the Reserves, since you couldn't be mobilized. I retired as a Colonel.

"Our family has always had close ties to the military. I've mentioned my dad's service. My wife's father was a West Point graduate. He graduated in the same class as President Eisenhower and several other generals. My son went to West Point for college and has remained in the Army. He graduated 29 years ago this year and is a Colonel serving in Afghanistan right now. And my grandson is a cadet at West Point.

"The kids have been around the military their whole lives. When I was in the California government, one of my duties was to have the Cabinet responsibility for the California National Guard. When our kids were little, I would go on my inspection trips, and I would take them along. They would live with me on the military post for a week every spring, and enjoy riding in jeeps. They also knew that I went off to military duty during the summer every year. It was just part of the routine of the family, to be involved in the military."

Meese talks about what other influences his children had in their lives to formulate their patriotism, beyond the military involvement.

"Our own kids would participate in activities related to what I was doing, or what my wife was doing, in our various activities. When my kids were little, and I would go to work on Saturdays, they would go with me and play in the halls outside the governor's office. All of those activities had to do a lot with government, and ignited their thinking about how the government worked, which contributed to their ideas about patriotism."

Meese talks about what parents can do to help instill patriotism in their own kids, since most of them won't be playing in the halls of the governor's office.

"What can parents do to help their kids learn about patriotism? A lot of it is reading; read to them or have them read. When I was growing up there were a lot of books that had patriotic themes, books about the history of the United States. Again, it was a part of life. It is important for young people to learn about history, about the founding, and about the way in which the country came to be, about the early days of the colonists, and the Constitution. All of this information is vital to understanding the foundation of patriotism and why this country is special and why serving the country and participating in civic activities should be important elements of patriots' daily lives.

"One of the problems in our modern society is too often there's an emphasis on what's *wrong* with our country instead of what is *great* about the country.

"There are a lot of books that are very interesting for young people. For example, Frank Keating, the former governor of Oklahoma, has written several books for young people about our history, about Theodore Roosevelt, Standing Bear and Will Rogers. They make for very interesting reading.

"There are also organizations that are particularly good at teaching about government and citizenship too.

"When I was in high school, I went to a Junior Statesmen school, which was a six-week program during the summer, between my junior and senior year. There, they had college-type courses for high school kids at a camp-type arrangement. They had courses in public speaking, American government and leadership. They actually organized a government for the students in which each student participated in different roles of government during the course of the six weeks. I've been on the Junior Statesmen Board for 40 years; they have them in many high schools all over the country. All my kids went through the program as did two of our grandchildren.

"The Young America's Foundation has a very good program for high school students and a particularly good one for college students. They also operate the Ronald Reagan Ranch Project, which includes a teaching center."

Asked about how parents can teach their kids about the founding documents, Meese talks about what he did to teach his kids.

"Because of my work, this topic came up frequently in dinner table conversation. All of our kids went through the Junior Statesmen School, so they learned through intensive courses on these kinds of things, and we augmented that in discussions at home.

"A lot of young people are getting taught like this, particularly with regard to American history and government, by parents who home-school their children. I've found that many of the people who are involved in home schooling are particularly dedicated to patriotism, love of country, an understanding of history and the Constitution. That's one of the reasons why many of them do home-school their kids."

Meese talks about what other things parents can do to get involved in their children's lives and influence them to be patriotic.

"Scouting organizations are very important. For our daughters and granddaughters, there are Girl Scouts, and for the fellows, Boy Scouts. My son and grandson were both Eagle Scouts. Part of this effort involves the parents participating in the scouting activities themselves, either with Boy Scouts for boys, or for the girls, either Campfire Girls or Girl Scouts.

"When I was in the Boy Scouts, once a year, there was Good Government Day. Scouts would get a day out of school so they could participate in various departments of local government. Scouts would sit with the judge in court or be with the police department or the fire department or some other department of government for a day. Everybody looked forward to that. Once you've done that, you naturally have a continuing interest in such things."

Being a patriot really teaches our kids important values and ideas. Meese tells what his take is on these values we are teaching our kids when we emphasize patriotism.

"It's a whole set of values. You teach kids about honesty, about helping others, about being friendly towards others, and accepting them. Patriotism is being willing to serve your government, your country, your community. All of these things are part of a continuum. You don't isolate patriotism as a single value. It's part of the total set of values that you have in a family. Having children understand the history of the country, and then relating that to their own lives is an important relationship. For example, children should learn how we help other countries. In Haiti and other places suffering from floods and fires and other tragedies, we've been very generous country in helping others. Likewise, within our own country, people help each other.

"It all starts with parents taking the time, and having an interest in being with their kids and imparting the culture and values to their children, and leading by personal example.

"I can remember, as a little kid, going with my dad when he was recruiting donations for the Red Cross. So much of what I learned was just being with my folks. My dad was the commander of the American Legion post. So, when they would have these Americanism days, my brothers and I would always go with him. We kind of picked up patriotism by 'osmosis.'

"It's also a matter of helping kids to understand that there are some things that have happened in our country's history that we're not awfully proud of. At the same time, they should learn that, basically, we are a good country, but even good countries sometimes make mistakes.

"People have different points of view regarding what is a good thing and what is a bad thing and one of the values of a country like ours is that you have people with different views, and they are free to express those views. We have a government where the majority rules, but it means that other people that have different views can try to persuade others to come to their point of view and change the majority.

"One of the most important things that we can teach children about is their duty of citizenship. In order for government to work in a free country, people have to be willing to accept responsibilities, not the least of which is voting. But it also means participating themselves. It may actually be serving in public office, or just helping other people who are serving an office. At the very least, it means learning what is going on in government and in the community."

★ ★ ★ *Key Points* ★ ★ ★

- Participate in government in some way, including your civic duty of voting. This illustrates to your children your commitment to the country.

- Teach your children real values—honesty, love of country, duty.

- It's a very strong relationship when children understand this country's history and relate it to their own lives.

- Consider Junior Statesman programs, Boy Scouts and Girl Scouts, and The Young America's Foundation's programs for your children.

- Have discussions with your children, such as at the dinner table.

- Read to your children and have them read interesting books about our history.

- Teach your children the duty of citizenship including voting, serving in public office or at least know what's going on in government and the community.

Chapter 11

HERITAGE

Charlie Rhoads

★ ★ ★ ★ ★

Charlie Rhoads is an entrepreneur, warrior, family man, and self-described "knowledge seeker." In addition to his business partnerships within Deep Blue Group, he also serves on the Board of Directors for the Joe Foss Institute, a charitable organization which promotes patriotism, integrity and public service. He is the Chairman of the Board at America's Mighty Warriors which rights injustices and cares for the troops and their families and the families of the fallen. Additionally he has been heavily involved with the Naval Special Warfare Foundation for many years. He is married to his high school sweetheart Lorraine and together they are the parents of a five-year-old son, a two-year old-daughter with a third on the way.

Rhoads' journey to become a strong patriot and warrior is fascinating. His family is deeply rooted in American history. He also had a mentor in his life who epitomized patriotism, even though he wasn't a natural-born American. Here, he tells the story of his rich heritage and how it affected his decision to patriotically serve our country and get involved in his many pursuits to support the military.

"My story starts with a man names Johann Nicholas Bohner. He came from Reichenbach, Germany and was a Hessian soldier.

"He was paid by the British to fight against a rag-tag group of rebels in this foreign land. He was in Trenton, New Jersey, fighting against this group of Continentals, led by this fellow, General George Washington.

"Bohner was chasing them when Christmas came, and being the good Germans they were, they consumed large quantities of beer and had a rough morning. Washington took advantage of this and crossed the Delaware River into Trenton. They fought Colonel Johann Raul and his group of Hessians there. And that didn't go so well for old Granddad.

"He became a prisoner in Lancaster, Pennsylvania and over the course of time, ended up pledging allegiance to what the Continentals were doing and fighting with them.

"He acquired a plot of land and became one of the four founding families of Northumberland County, Pennsylvania. My entire family has been from Northumberland County until me. I'm 11 generations descended from him and one of the first males in the family that I know *not* to be a farmer in that Pennsylvania Dutch territory.

"We've had people fight in all conflicts. They fought with the Pennsylvania Volunteers in the Civil War. One of my great, great, great uncles was at Andersonville Prison for 3 years—one of the South's prisons during the Civil War. My mom's dad, Edward William Charlton was from Pennsylvania. He ended up going into the Army in 1943 during

World War II. He was with the 3rd Army, 79th Infantry 314th Infantry Regiment Cannon Company. He landed at Normandy as one of the follow-up landings. He and his unit had traveled throughout France. He was killed by artillery fire in a counter-assault from the Nazis in August of 1944.

"My mom was 14 months old, an only child. She was from a Gold Star family and grew up without a dad. Her mom came from a large family so there were lots of farmers, a lot of family around there. My mom was always looked after by all the aunts and uncles. We had a very patriotic family with a lot of service, and a lot of hard work. A strong Protestant work ethic and German stoicism was central to our family. Our family sacrificed a lot and I grew up hearing and knowing about that.

"What did my mom do to raise me as patriot? She talked about our family history. She told me who my family was, where we came from, what was important to them, and why it was important. Having that family history was such an important part of developing that core sense of who I was. It provided a sturdy foundation on which I could depend.

"My mom also instilled in me a deep sense of tradition. We lived in Arizona, and we would go back to Pennsylvania and Washington, DC, every other year. We would visit the family and we would always go back to this little cemetery at Himmel's Church in Rebuck, Pennsylvania.

"There's this big hill that rises from the church with all these tombstones. What I loved was that we would walk up to the oldest tombstones that were all chalky and falling apart with dates from the 1600's and early 1700's. I can see every generation of my family, as I walk up the hill, all the way up to where my mom already has her lot purchased.

"Seeing my great, great, great grandfather all the way to my grandfather and my grandmother and where they're buried and seeing the veteran's organizations coming out and putting flags out there on the major holidays is always awe-inspiring. We would always go and leave flowers there and we would talk about them.

"Going to DC always made it very real for me as well: going to the White House, the Capital, the Vietnam Veterans Memorial, even Mount Vernon. Mount Vernon was very, very special for our family because my mom's dad met my mom's mom when they were standing on the porch of Mount Vernon. He was in his ROTC uniform. A love affair began from there.

"The first time we took our son to Pennsylvania and Washington, DC, he was 2 years old. We wanted him to have pictures of himself standing at the Jefferson Memorial when he's two-years-old, to say, 'This is important.' In 20 years, he can look back on that and say, 'Yeah, that was important.' We take pictures with the headstones, with Grandma and with the other family members so there's this on-going body of what is important."

"We have these traditions. We travel to places. We always do something meaningful, regardless of where we go. We always hit those kinds of places as we traveled around the United States. It became a core part of our family."

Rhoads gave his suggestions about how much family tradition plays into raising strong patriots. Starting these traditions, when your children are very young, helps build their knowledge and understanding of patriotism. Strong traditions are important for patriotic families.

"If you don't have traditions, start making them up. Start communicating what's important," says Rhoads.

Beyond just moms and dads, Rhoads says, the entire family unit influences our children and how they feel about their country.

"It wasn't just parents for me. Parents, by far, have the most influence on a kid, who they are and who they're going to become. It's unfortunate that a lot of parents are stepping away and allowing other people, who don't have the vested interest that parents should have in their child, to do the teaching. The parent has so much influence, regardless if they are getting the feedback from the child.

"There's a parental role and there's a family role. Values also come from other people in the family, whether it's over generations or the same generation. There's definitely the family dynamic.

"My wife Lorraine's mom is number 6 of 12 kids. Her grandfather was one of four brothers, and none of those brothers had fewer than five kids. We're talking about a HUGE family. They all served in one capacity or another. Her grandfather, Bill Hebets, was in World War II in the Army in Europe. He fought at the Battle of the Bulge. The story of his valor has been told to each generation, who now believe 'Country' and 'Family' and 'Patriotism' are really important."

It is not only blood relations who influence our kids. This means it is important to take extra care and seek out the kinds of influences you want for your kids. Rhoads believes mentors are vital. Here he tells the story of his mentor's life. It is captivating.

"The third component is really important and often times forgotten. More valued in previous generations, having a mentor is invaluable. As a kid, having a mentor is vitally important, because we are preprogrammed to discount what our parents say but we will listen to an independent third party. I had someone who was and always will be probably one of the most important people in my entire life. His name was Conrad Braaten.

"You want to talk about patriotism? Write a book about *this* guy. He actually wrote his own book called *Beyond Madagascar* but it only briefly touched upon what an incredible human being he was. He was born to Norwegian and American missionary parents in Fort Dauphin, Madagascar. He grew up in Madagascar speaking Malagasy, French, Swahili, Norwegian and English. He spoke five languages as a child.

"He ended up in the United States and attended the University of Arizona to study political science. I later would attend the same university to study political science, following in his footsteps.

"One day in 1938, before he finished taking his course work, the president and the provost of the university pulled him out of class and said 'You need to come with us.' They went to the president's office. Inside were a couple of men from the United States government. They asked him if he was related to Olaf Braaten and others who ended up being in the Norwegian Underground during World War II. He said, 'Yes, those are my relatives.'

"They said, 'You were recommended to us and we need to ask you a few questions.' They said, 'The United States needs you. There's a major effort and we need you.' By this time, he spoke 7 languages fluently.

"'The United States needs you. We can't tell you what you might be doing, but it might mean putting your life on the line. Would you be willing to do that?' They told him.

"He said 'Can I think about it?' and they said, 'Sure, you've got a few minutes.' So he came back and sais, 'My dad is going to be deeply disappointed that I haven't finished my school.' The men spoke for a moment and the president came back and said, 'Congratulations!'

"He ended up becoming part of the Office of Strategic Services (OSS) which was the precursor to the Central Intelligence Agency (CIA) and Special Forces. He operated in the tunnels in Europe for several years during World War II doing things like you would see in the Jason Bourne movies, against the Nazis and the Schutzstaffel (SS.) He then became a counter intelligence officer in East Germany from 1945 to about 1955.

"His wife developed a very severe case of viral meningitis. The doctor said, 'She's going to die. There's nothing we can do for her. You need to be with her through the last night.'

"And he prayed. He prayed all through the night. In the morning, he came back to her room and she was surrounded by doctors and nurses, sitting up eating breakfast. The doctor was shaking his head saying, 'It's a miracle. She should be dead.'

"Throughout his evening of prayer, Conrad Braaten had made a promise with God and said, 'If you let her live, I will quit the US Army and I will go to seminary and become a pastor.'

"He held true to his promise and resigned his commission, went to seminary and became a Lutheran pastor. He was the pastor at Ascension Lutheran Church in Scottsdale, Arizona. My mom was attending church where he was the pastor so I got to know him.

"He baptized and confirmed me, was a mentor to me. He married my wife and me, and was there for our kids' births. He helped found the World Brotherhood Exchange. He worked with Billy Graham and the Kennedys. He was just a dialed-in individual. What a great human being.

"He taught me how to shoot. He taught me about integrity, patriotism and about how to be a good man and a good husband. He taught me how to be everything that I am.

"He died about a year and a half ago after a struggle with cancer. That was probably one of the most difficult days of my life. His legacy is alive and well and I will continue to spread the word about who he was as an individual. He had a tremendous impact on my life and was a fantastic mentor. I'll forever owe him a debt of gratitude.

"Mentors are huge. John Greer, Tom Coulter, Jim Hebets, and others, all played huge roles in my life. Another mentor of mine was CAPT Roger Meek. He's now the Chief Staff Officer for a SEAL Group in Coronado, California. What a phenomenal mentor, leader and human being. A lot of my friends had some fantastic mentors both in and out of the Navy. That's kind of where my conception of what patriotism is comes from."

Although Rhoads' children are still young, he and his wife have already started working to instill a love of this country and knowledge of its deep history in their kids. The Rhoads family has a very specific plan as they establish their own family traditions, and combine their family heritage to pass these along to their children.

"We really came down to looking at this in three ways. First, we needed to have a philosophy that we believed in. We knew we needed to communicate something to our kids about this, but didn't know where to start.

"So we decided we needed to come up with the content of what we wanted to communicate, what we wanted to teach. We needed to be able to explain what our philosophy was so we started our own family book. We went out to an Italian paper company named Epica that creates these old leather-bound books that have parchment-like paper. When you get the book, it looks like it is 500 years old!

"We said 'This is our family book.' We created our own family crest, our family's mission statement, family vision, our core values and philosophies, rules we govern ourselves by and our goals and our dreams. These were all different chapters in the family book. We continue to add to it.

"As the kids get older, as we become smarter and more mature, and as things come up, we can change it. It's very much an organic thing. We started to put it together and we said we needed a philosophy. From there, we defined things that are important to us. Some of the content, the traditions, I learned from my own mom.

Rhoads says it is important to make these experiences tactile, something they see, feel and remember. He and his wife take great steps to allow their children to be involved in local events so they can really understand and learn what it is like to be an American patriot.

"We'll get books and show them this is what's important about the United States and what's so special about our unique set of liberties that are a guiding light in the world. Sometimes the light dims. We aren't perfect but we are a guiding light. We stick with those core philosophies of freedom and service to others and personal liberty and sacrifice.

"I think for a kid, it's so important to have that experiential understanding. They're going to better remember these philosophies if they go to a patriotic parade and they see the fire trucks and they see the people marching in the parade. Little community parades are so important.

"When we go to San Diego and see my friends in the Navy, in uniform. My son asks, 'What are they doing?' and I tell him, 'Freedom comes at a price. These are the people that are standing the watch. These are Daddy's friends.' That has an impact right there. It's not only verbal communication, but also experience, whether it's going to the memorials or parades or air shows. It's a slice of Americana. It goes back to those traditions."

Rhoads says even at his son's young age, he is already starting to understand our history and ask questions about who was important and why.

"'Dad,' he said, 'I have a very, very important question for you— Who is the most important leader in the country?'

"I said, 'Ever or right now?'

"He says, 'Well, ever, Dad. Who's the most important leader?'

"I said, 'There's been a lot of important leaders. Without a lot of them, we wouldn't have today. My own personal thought is that George Washington is the most important.'

"He asked, 'Why?'

"It gave me an opportunity to talk to him about what could have happened if it hadn't been for people who said, 'I don't want to be a king. I'm only going to do this twice.'

"Then my son said, 'What was so special about George Washington? Was he a great patriot because he led the Continental Army?'

'Yeah.' I said.

'Was he a great patriot because he was the president?'

'Yeah.'

"He was getting it; he understood the information swimming around in his head so now he was thinking, 'This is someone who's important to my dad.'

"By asking questions and listening to their responses, you can see the information sinking in.

'Well, who are some others?' he asked.

"That gave me the opportunity to tell him about other great leaders out there. Now, I'll hear him saying 'Four score and seven years ago...' He was so excited when he figured out that meant 87 years. He was going around telling everyone about Abraham Lincoln!

"One of the most powerful things he said to me was when we were standing in front of the Vietnam Veterans Memorial in Washington, DC. My wife was holding our daughter. He was standing there for a long time, and he was quiet. He turned around and he looked completely ashen and he said, 'Dad, this is a lot of names...Dad, a lot of people died.'

"He was five years old.

"That's why I'm such a fan of that kind of experience. There's no number of books, or anything that you could say that will have that kind of impact on a kid."

Rhoads makes sure his family goes to visit all the important American landmarks on family vacations. Again, the experience helps the information sink in and ties what they have learned back to something real instead of just hearing a story. He talks about how much he also learns and remembers by going, so it is not just for the kids; parents can learn and relearn history too.

"We've been to the Smithsonian, the National Archives, Independence Hall in Philadelphia, Williamsburg, Virginia, Monticello, Mount Vernon. It affords us the opportunity to talk about what was so unique about the Constitution and the Declaration of Independence, for example.

"What was so unique about the Declaration of Independence was the fact that these signers gave up everything for this idea of freedom. Unlike other rebel groups in other lands, they had lands, riches, businesses. They committed treason to provide liberty, gave it all up for freedom.

"Every time we go and made these trips, I learn so much, too. I think I took more away from these trips than my kids.

"It inspires me. How incredible, how forward-thinking it was to do what they did, and say what they said the way they said it. To craft and construct a body of language that would offer light to so many people in our country, and throughout the world, and would be there for us in our moments of need as a country, when things are very bad and there's internal dissention, was truly brilliant.

"Even though the Founding Fathers didn't always live by the core concepts and principles, they knew where this country was supposed to go, what it was supposed to be about and what was important to the people. It is so incredibly powerful to think about the way that they did what they did and how they thought about all the necessary mechanisms that have to be in place to ensure there wouldn't be a tyranny of any branch of government, to have the checks and balances systems and due process clause, and spelling out the inalienable rights that we have. Their knowledge definitely had to have had some kind of otherworldly influence.

"To have the world as it is today because of that divine guidance, to have the body of knowledge available to all people, to have the freedom to question things, and to educate ourselves and to come out of darkness, is invaluable. The exponential amount of information that is out there today is because of that, because of those documents, and because of the people who put their lives on the line and signed their lives away to support and defend us. That's not just the Founding Fathers but many, many generations of patriots and citizens, soldiers and warriors ever since then."

As a former Navy veteran still heavily involved in military support organizations, Rhoads has very strong ideas about patriotism and what it means to be an American compared to an American patriot.

"Every citizen of the United States should be a patriot. Not all of them are, that's for sure. In terms of thinking about patriots, I've kind of always broken them out in my mind in a couple of different ways.

"Citizen patriots don't have to go into the military or have a family member who has done that. They just need to feel blessed that they're in this country and support and defend what's important and what's not, amongst their social circles. Too many people have been too meek about that and not expressing, 'Hey, that's what I believe in. Here's what's important to me.' That's patriotism right there, supporting our country's national interest, both at home or abroad.

"Another kind of patriot is a soldier. Soldiers have families and other goals in life and they're serving because they need money for college or they feel called to do that, but it might not be their life-calling. That's a little bit different kind of patriot. They may be trying to get out of a bad set of circumstances, a bad neighborhood, or a bad situation. There are a lot of stresses, risks and sacrifices that come from being a soldier, sailor, airman, Marine, or Coast Guardsman.

"Then there's the warrior patriot. A warrior patriot doesn't care about the politics of what they are doing or why they are doing it. That's not their position. They signed that blank check, payable to the United States government, for an amount up to, and including, their life, if necessary.

"They do that because that's who they are. Everything in their core says, 'This country, this way of life, these people, this family, are so important to me, I'm going to go out and put my body, my mind, my soul, everything, out there. I am going to take it to the limit. I'm going to tap into that and do whatever it takes, at all cost. If that means sacrificing my life, so be it.' For these types of people, there's no glory in that. They don't want medals. They don't want to be lauded. They don't want any of that. They want to go out and know they did what they were called to do.

"That's where I came from. Growing up, I always felt called. I wanted to be a frogman when I was four years old. I discussed this with my mentor many times, that calling. He would tell me these stories about World War II, about guys who signed up and lied about their ages so they could serve at age 14. I thought, 'That's a really good idea.

I'm going to go do that.' So I went into the Naval recruiting station in Scottsdale, Arizona, and said 'I want to be a frogman. A SEAL. I want to be a warrior.' I was 14.

"I went in and I talked to a Chief Crozier—he was a submarine machinist main chief. I walked in there and I said, 'I want to sign up.' And he said, 'How old are you?' I said, 'Uh, I'm 18.' 'How old are you really?' he asked. 'I'm 14, but I'm willing to lie,' was my response. He laughed at me and said, 'Son, that's great, but that's not going to happen. Come back in 4 years and we'll talk.'

"He told me to talk to a guy in the Sea Cadet program—United States Naval Sea Cadet Corps (NSCC). I became a sea cadet. I spent years as a sea cadet and I loved it. I spent my summers out at sea, on board the *U.S.S. Frederick*, among others. I had a great time.

"The US Navy League sponsored this program for kids. It was kind of like Junior ROTC but the participants are actually on board the ships, doing the job with the real soliders. That taught me a lot.

"NSCC is a great program for developing patriots. Cub Scouts and Boy Scouts are a great program for teaching kids a lot of the core fundamentals of leadership, patriotism, integrity and public service. If your child has an interest in going into a particular service, especially in this case, the Navy or the Marine Corps, Sea Cadets is a fantastic program. Your child can actually go out and get a running mate, a real guy on a real ship, and get those experiences in as a kid.

"Four years later, when I was old enough, I went back to that same recruiting station. Chief Crozier was still there. I enlisted as a parachute rigger in the Divefarer SEAL training pipeline.

"That passionate, warrior-like brand of patriotism is what I talk to my kids about, probably more than what the average is because I've got my friends and others who are out putting their lives on the line, on that watch."

★ ★ ★ *Key Points* ★ ★ ★

- Learn about your family's history and heritage, where they came from, what was important to them and why. The stories will have a strong effect on your children. Visit where your ancestors are from in the country for a bigger impact.

- Find a trusted mentor for your child, a third party voice to be an influence. Also utilize other family members beyond parents like aunts and uncles.

- Even at the earliest age, talk to your kids about history and take them to historical places such as the Smithsonian, the National Archives, Independence Hall, Williamsburg, Virginia, Monticello and Mount Vernon.

- Consider making a book about your family's values and philosophy, mission statement, rules and goals, and include your photographs for a historical record. If you don't have any of ideas or traditions, start some.

- Go to patriotic events, like community parades for a more tactile experience for your children.

- Visit military sites and talk about how soldiers keep us safe.

- Check out the Sea Cadet program for real life military experience as well as Boy Scouts and Girl Scouts for teaching fundamental values.

- Remember patriotism has many faces—citizen, soldier, and warrior.

Chapter 12

DEBATE

Seth Swirsky

★ ★ ★ ★ ★

Seth Swirsky is an award-winning singer and songwriter, as well an author, blogger, artist, filmmaker, baseball fanatic and Beatles fan. He co-wrote the 80s hit "*Tell it To My Heart*" performed most famously by Taylor Dayne, as well as many other great hits. He is the author of several books including *Something to Write Home About*, the third book in a trilogy of books that are comprised of letters written to Seth from professional baseball players. He and his wife, Jody, live in Beverly Hills, California with their children—two sons and one daughter.

Swirsky grew-up as the child of young parents in the 1960s. He was an activist on the liberal side of the spectrum for many years because of his "indoctrination," as he calls it, against things that were pro-American and patriotic. Here Seth talks a bit about his upbringing,

127

which is an excellent example of how much passion we can instill in our kids at a very young age, in either direction, either loving or disparaging this country.

"My parents were Democrats, but not hard-core Democrats—they voted for JFK in 1960, the year I was born. The sixties made up the wallpaper of my life. It was beautiful because when you're a very young kid - 5 in 1965, 7 in 1967- you saw Jimi Hendrix posters. They were all electric, and they looked amazing. You heard the music: it was so melodic, and sounded great. I didn't have to worry about being drafted. I didn't have to make a decision about 'do I take LSD or not?' I wasn't 16. I was 7. I got all the optimism of it, without it being a political thing, like, 'We're going to raze the Pentagon.' All that cultural stuff was really poisonous in many ways, but I didn't know that then. I got the best of the sixties, the absolute best.

"I didn't know what it meant when my babysitters came over and their t-shirts said, 'End the draft' and all that stuff. I didn't know what the Columbia University shut down was about. I was only seven years old.

"When I entered sixth grade in 1971, I started writing letters to politicians. Just recently, I found one I had written to President Nixon. I was 10 years old. It said, 'How dare you send our troops to Vietnam when you're not even sending your daughters' husbands there, and your daughters are not even serving. How dare you!' So, there I was this little budding, angry, anti-Right, leftist that my teacher's were quite proud of. My teachers and community encouraged my 'all-things-Republican-are-evil' bias.

"When I was in sixth grade, we had a big debate where my teacher chose countries or continents to compare and contrast. They included India, China, Africa and Japan (of course *not* The United States!). She chose the leading students in the class to be the heads of each of the countries. I was chosen to be the head of China and prove that China was the best country in the world in which to live. Can you believe? Chairman Mao was a figure to be looked up to —not, as I discovered in adulthood, a man who massacred upwards of 60 million of his own people. That was not in my textbook in my preparation for the debate about how great China was. By the way, the China team, of which I headed, won the debate."

Seth's older child attends a well-known liberal high school in Santa Monica, California, where he is a very rare breed, a young, America-loving conservative. Swirsky speaks proudly of how his son has become his own person at a young age and how he confidently stands up for his beliefs, even when it pits him against his mostly leftist teachers and his friends.

"I'm thrilled that my son goes to the school he goes to. I believe it is a unique opportunity for him to know what he's going to be up against in the overwhelmingly, liberal-dominated media centers in the country, where he is likely to live and have a business. He is already a very successful musician and producer, but he is going to be challenged by a lot of people in New York and Los Angeles, and around the world. It's not a bad thing to have practice defending your beliefs at a young age.

"The other day, he was in a social studies class, and his teacher said to him, 'You don't believe in hate speech,' referring to someone's criticism of radical Islam vis-à-vis the wars in Iraq and Afghanistan? And he said, 'Don't you think that people should be able to voice their opinions? If people don't like those opinions, they don't have to subscribe to them. Doesn't a critic have the protection of the First Amendment? Isn't this country based on the freedom of speech? What makes this country unique is the First Amendment and standing up for it!'

"He's very, very proud of his conservatism and yet he is an extremely popular kid at a very leftist school, and more often than not, he has kids coming back to him -- his friends and many teachers, who keep quiet about their own conservatism—saying things like, 'you really opened my eyes to another way of thinking that we don't get at this school. Thank you!' He is a real leader at 14, 15, or 16 years old.

"He understands that the whole raison d'etre behind liberalism is the 'victims vs. oppressors' mentality. He just (thankfully) doesn't buy it and is forthright in combating that 'idea.'"

Swirsky talks about what influence he may have had on his son's opinions, as well as how he taught him to think for himself, not just mimic his father.

"Many times when my son comes to me with his own ideas that run counter with mine, I initially applaud it as a way of allowing him to form his own ideas. There is always time to debate the issue, but it's important to allow your child to get to their own ideas in their own way first, allowing their own thought processes to develop. In the end, I've tried to get him to use a common sense approach in forming his own worldview.

"He loves our country, and understands his opinions are his own. For instance, somebody recently said to him, 'It's terrible what happened with slavery, and there's got to be justice today.' His retort was, 'Do you understand that 650,000 Americans died fighting the Civil War to correct the mistake of slavery?' He's also very aware that our soldiers in the fields of Afghanistan and Iraq are fighting for many reasons, not the least of which is our ultimate freedom. He's very patriotic."

Swirsky also has two younger children. Here he talks about how he has started to teach them about loving their country.

"With small children, I keep it small and I keep it symbolic. For instance, we have an American flag that flies outside of our house. It gives me an opportunity to talk about the flag and why I want to display it, which leads to more conversations about why we are an exceptional country. I tell them we are exceptional because, with this flag as our countries symbol, we have helped save and promote freedom. I tell them this is a good and well-meaning country, a country of high morals whose soldiers fight not only for the right of its people to live in freedom, but so that those in other countries, such as Iraq, can as well.

"I put a photograph of President Lincoln in-between my little girl's room and my little boy's room, and I tell them about Lincoln and what he did for our country. There is also a photograph of George Washington. I keep it somewhat basic, so I can talk about the person once they ask. Once their interest is sparked, we start reading more about some great Americans and what they have contributed to the world.

"It's a slow approach. Now my 8 year-old son is excited by the presidents, like I was at that age. It came about because he saw pictures of and heard about the presidents and all they accomplished."

Swirsky also spoke about how he keeps the discussion going with all the kids.

"I try and foster debate every night at my dinner table. I say, 'What's a current event that we could talk about today?' It doesn't have to be about the death penalty, per se, with a six-year-old, an eight-year-old and a 16-year-old. For example, I asked the kids, 'Hey, did you read that story about that kid who had an American flag, and the principal said he couldn't display it while he was riding his bicycle?' Then the kids said, 'Hey, Dad. We have an American flag. Does that mean we have to take it down?' I said, 'No, that means we have to keep it up!! That means that we have to support this boy. This boy was saying what we're saying. We love our country. We have nothing to be ashamed of in our love and support of our country. We must fight against those who say that you can't show that respect through the display of our flag!

"Around-the-dinner-table conversations are very important. The topic doesn't always have to be provocative, but there are important issues that show up in the news sometimes and parents should not be afraid to bring these up in conversation."

Swirsky sees debate as good, exactly what the Founders wanted. If his son, or your child runs up against another child—or teacher—who doesn't simply name-call, but debates, that's a good thing.

"I teach my kids to be able to back-up what they are saying with hard, cold facts, to really think about your position, and don't be afraid to stand up for what you believe in.

"My older son has asked me, 'Dad, what if someone presents an answer to one of my ideas that trumps one of my debate points? I said to him, 'Good. If he tells you something that you didn't know, and it sounds credible, and he cites it from a credible resource, you can say, "Thank you for showing me that."'

In describing what he thinks is the most important concept or big idea to teach children about being a patriot, Swirsky has a simple answer.

"The most important responsibility is to protect our freedoms, so 'freedom' is the operative word I use in my house. It's all about freedom: If you want to say something that's controversial, you should be able to say it without the threat of repercussions. Unfettered 'Freedom' is the blood flow that runs through the veins of a healthy America!"

★ ★ ★ *Key Points* ★ ★ ★

- Foster your children's own opinions by encouraging them to think through *why* they hold their opinion, *then* share your opinion.

- Fly the American flag. Talk about its history and why you are proud to display it.

- Talk about the presidents with young children.

- Talk about how our soldiers fight for our country and our freedoms and also fight for the freedoms of people in other countries.

- Discuss current events at the dinner table, at the right level for your children.

- Debate is good—it is part of the foundation of our country. Don't let your children feel intimidated by the possibility of having a debate.

- Freedom is the backbone of this nation—teach your kids to fight for their freedom.

Chapter 13

KNOWLEDGE

Janine Turner

Janine Turner is an actress, author, singer and the co-founder of Constituting America, a non-profit organization dedicated to spreading knowledge about America's founding documents. She authored the book *Holding Her Head High: 12 Single Mothers Who Championed Their Children and Changed History*, a spiritual and historical account of 12 mothers who were abandoned, widowed or divorced, and the impact they had on their children's lives as well as the course of history. She is the mother of one daughter.

Turner's family has a rich history in this country, one deeply involved in the military and the Christian church. Here she gives a little background about her family and how she learned about this country's history.

"My father is from Athens, Texas. He was this very bright and athletic child. He graduated in 1957 from the United States Military Academy at West Point. He chose the Air Force because he wanted to fly. He is one of few esteemed people to fly twice the speed of sound. I was raised with jets flying over my head. I am sure that had some sort of subliminal impact on me.

"My father was always a highly moral person, as was my mother, who led their lives in a very dignified manner. That, along with a strong family heritage of faith, played a part in the innate impact on me as a child. My great grandmother, on my mother's side, was a pillar of the Baptist Church. She played the piano and was very, very active in the church. My grandfather's father was a Methodist preacher."

Turner talks about how she developed her fascination with our country's foundational principles and the Founders themselves.

"I just had a great interest in the Founding Fathers since I was a young girl. I remember asking my father, when I was in third grade, 'Dad, if our Founding Fathers were to come back today, what would they be most disappointed about?' He thought about it for a while, then he looked at me and said, 'Taxes.' It's obviously probably a much more complex answer now. And now that I've studied *The Federalist Papers*, I realize it really is more. They would be *very* disappointed in the scope and breadth and size of our government.

"As a child, I always loved to read biographies. I would sit down by the lower shelf of the library and dig out all the biographies. Even as a young child, if I was going to read, I wanted it to be something that was really stimulating for me. I wasn't reading a lot of novels.

"I also have to give credit to my fifth grade teacher, who was my all-time favorite teacher at my elementary school in Fort Worth, Texas. It was his first year as a teacher. It was my first year in this particular school district. In fifth grade, you are supposed to study the Constitution and the Revolutionary era but he decided to take the whole year and study the year 1776. We put on the musical, *1776*. That took my whole fascination with our Founding Fathers to a higher realm. If I could say anything to parents, it would be to purchase the musical, *1776*, and make sure you watch it with your children on July 4th, if not throughout the year. It's fantastic."

In addition to parents, Turner stresses that there are teachers in the United States who are trying to emphasize our founding principles and teach them to our kids. She has witnessed this first hand throughout her travels.

"Teachers also have a huge impact. Our country's history is not being taught with the same reverence and dignity as it used to be.

"I traveled 6,200 miles this year in this very small RV to film the winners of our Constituting America 9/17 contest with my co-chair, Cathy Gillespie and my daughter. Some winners were home schooled. Some winners attended Christian schools. Some winners attended public schools.

"These days, people tend to think that all teachers are against the Constitution and our Founding Fathers. And we found that not to be true. There are some very brave school principals and teacher out there who are determined to teach their children the real blessings that we reaped because of our Founding Fathers. I give them high kudos and applaud them for really embracing our Constitution."

Beyond our children's educations, Turner also encourages parents to be actively involved in their children's school and extracurricular activities to make sure their kids are being exposed to the founding principles and documents that helped make this country great.

"It's the squeaky wheel that gets the grease. Be an active, involved parent. Ask if the children are allowed to say the Pledge of Allegiance.

Ask what the children are being taught and how the teachers are teaching the Constitution. By law, schools are supposed to talk about and teach the Constitution on September 17th—Constitution Day. Frequently, however, teachers are oblivious of the law, principals don't enforce it, and this day of focus is ignored. Parents can really make a difference just by being inquisitive."

Turner talks about what parents can do to be sure their children know it is ok to grow-up thinking about and studying our history and founding documents as a part of their after-school activities, like sports and the arts. She says so much emphasis is put on becoming famous through athletics or the arts, instead of simply learning how to be a good American.

"This is ironic, coming from me, because I'm an actress and a singer. My daughter loves to sing, and we do albums together. My father was an athlete and played football in college. Having said that, there is this incredible emphasis today on the wrong things. Our children are born, and people express their hopes, saying, 'Hey, maybe he'll be a football star,' or, 'Maybe our daughter will be a singer.' Reality shows, *American Idol,* and football games seem to have eclipsed the importance of being a patriot.

"During the revolutionary era, and after the war was won, parents were realizing that their children were the future of the country. They wanted to educate them, teach them, and have them be proud of their heritage. We've lost that because we get involved in television, gossip, and the arts more than we should. I'm trying to encourage my daughter to balance this. There has to be fun for the children, but also an appreciation of the education that our forefathers had.

"For example, I've been reading Abigail Adam's biography. John Adams wrote to Abigail Adams and said something like, 'I need to make sure I've done enough thinking today.' My daughter and I will talk about this because I'm actually home schooling her this year. We'll say, 'Have we done enough thinking and studying today?' Together we relish the wealth of opportunities that we have and resources to educate ourselves.

"I like to joke and say that instead of putting a football in little babies' hands when they're born, or a microphone for girls, we need to put the Constitution in their hands. It's never too early to start teaching them.

"When your kids are four, five or six, start reading the Constitution, and talking about it around the dinner table. Make it a part of the tradition of family get-togethers. It starts at home. Just to make this part of the family discussion is one of the best ways to bring this topic to the forefront. Start early and never stop. The goal of parents today is to make sure, when your child is a teenager and someone mentions the Constitution, your kid doesn't say, 'Constitution, huh? What?'

"What we're trying to do is re-weave this into our cultural tapestry, so Americans are consciously aware of our rights and the relevance of the Constitution.

"We need to teach our kids that this is not an antiquated document. It's very, very relevant. We have a whole forum on the *Constituting America* website about *The Federalist Papers*. We had scholars who explained the Constitution and *The Federalist Papers*. I wrote 90 essays about how the Constitution is relevant today. Parents should brush up on these, too.

"Our country is at a crossroads now. Our children need to understand that they are the torchbearers of our liberties. The Bill of Rights, all of our amendments, the structure of government that we live and breathe today, must be known and understood by our children if they are to understand when their rights are being slowly usurped from them.

"My daughter and I are starting patriot clubs. We want kids all across America to be involved in these patriot clubs. Get a group of kids together, talk about the Constitution, talk about the Founding Fathers, and then regroup on the *Constituting America* website and discuss your club's activities in our forum. Parents will have to spearhead getting their kids involved. There are a lot of interested kids in high school and college. We are starting these patriot clubs meeting once a month to really talk about the country and the founding principles, and how they apply to today."

I asked Janine what she thinks her daughter would say to me if I asked her why she loves this country and what makes it so special.

"I would think she would say this country is special because of the absolute brilliance of our forefathers, and because its existence truly is a miracle. She's written her own little speeches about how winning the Revolutionary War was a miracle, as was the writing of the Constitution, about how smart Alexander Hamilton was and so were George Washington, John Adams, James Madison and Thomas Jefferson. She talks about how we were founded on such profound principles, which included the great liberties afforded us: the freedom to succeed or to fail, religious freedom, freedom to petition, so many freedoms. She loves the First Amendment, which she has made up a little acronym for: RAPPS - Freedom of Religion, Freedom to Assemble, Freedom of the Press, Freedom to Petition, and Freedom of Speech.

"She would say that this country gives her the opportunity to grow-up and be whoever she wants to be. She would also say that she's very afraid of the debt. She's very obsessed with the debt and where we're going with that. She wants to go to law school and go into politics."

Turner spoke about how she and her daughter discuss the founding documents on their many long drives back and forth from her daughter's dance class. They have lots of time to talk about all of these things.

"I drive her to ballet everyday because she's dancing five days a week. That's a three-hour trek, an hour and a half in, and an hour and a half back. She reads out loud to me from her American History book. And we love it. We highlight and we recap. She 'squares' any word she doesn't know. It's just been a lot of fun to study together. And it's expanding our knowledge from what we've already learned about *The Federalist Papers* and the Constitution. I also think that participating in contests like what we have through *Constituting America*, meeting all the other kids, corresponding with other children who also love the Founding Fathers, has really been fun for her as well.

"She is proud to be an American. She wants to preserve America so that it can be the great country that it is in the future."

Asked what the most significant contribution parents can make when they are raising their kids to be good patriots, Turner had a solid answer.

"Knowledge.

"I hearken back, of course, to our Founding Fathers, our founding principles, our Constitution, our Declaration of Independence, our history, how relevant these things are today, the sacrifices made by all people in American history, fighting to preserve our freedoms. But, I don't believe most people have an appreciation for what we have. That may be our biggest obstacle to overcome with today's generation: they just have no sense of appreciation for the sacrifices people have made for this country. They also don't have any sort of awareness of the danger that our republic is in. It all stems from a lack of education. Not really a lack of caring, but a lack of education. Knowledge is the most important element in raising a patriot, and it is the parent's responsibility to make sure that their children receive that knowledge.

"Really activate your child's mind, encourage them, take them to museums, take them to plays, create patriot clubs, have them join debate teams, make history fun for them, and really encourage them to get involved in government in any way where they can reach-out and go beyond themselves. All of these experiences are very valuable."

Turner speaks about why teaching a child to be a patriot is important.

"It empowers the children. It encourages them and creates active citizens. One cannot read about our history, our Founding Fathers, the great documents and the republic, without having this flame come alive and to want to make a difference. It's like Kennedy's quote, 'Ask not what your country can do for you, but what you can do for your country.' It gives them a sense of purpose, to realize that they are not victims, to know they are not powerless, and that they do have a hand in their own destiny. The worst thing in the world is to have an apathetic child who feels frightened and powerless. One of the greatest values in creating a patriot is realizing a sense of empowerment to go out and be a leader.

"I wrote an essay where I talked about the fact that Americans have gotten lazy. We took a nap on the beach. Then this tsunami came, and we are awakening again, similar to the enlightenment of the Revolution, accompanied by an awakening of the knowledge of our God-given rights. If we could teach our children anything, it's that God gives us our rights, not government.

"Our Founding Fathers wanted government to be very much contained in a box. They reviewed with great detail, and with providence or a hand from God, and developed this wonderful system of checks and balances, to ensure that government would remain small, an important aspect of the plan that seems to have been lost in today's government.

"We cannot be discouraged. The great thing is we still can make a difference right now. It starts with us teaching our children, but more importantly, it starts with us being examples to our children. If they see us as concerned citizens, volunteering, reaching out, being a part of campaigns, attending rallies, studying *The Federalist Papers*, reading history, if they see us doing these things then they will be inspired to say, 'Wait a minute, these are the footsteps I need to follow.'

"We want unity in our country, but the faction is what keeps us from becoming a monarchy or living under a dictatorship. James Madison really fostered faction because he thought that was the only way that there wouldn't be a monopoly of one party. As he said, 'Liberty is to faction what air is to fire.'

"We should not be discouraged by this political world that seems so nasty and horrible, because it was just as bad during the revolutionary times. In a way, that's kind of the beauty of democracy. We need to unite and come together and have that revolutionary fervor again to enlighten our children and save our country. The biggest issue is going to be with our economy, and we are all going to have to make sacrifices financially, especially with cutbacks that are coming. The more that we can brave this with a vision of preserving our country, the better."

★ ★ ★ *Key Points* ★ ★ ★

- Make history fun. Watch the musical *1776* with your children. Go to museums. Encourage them to join the debate team.

- Encourage them to get involved in government to move outside of themselves and help the community.

- Read the Constitution and other important documents, and make this a part of your daily family discourse daily. Make sure they learn the Bill of Rights, the Amendments and how our government is structured.

- Remember RAPPS for the First Amendment (Freedom of Religion, Assembly, Press, Petition and Speech).

- Stress to your children that God gave us our rights, not the government.

- Think enough each day, as John Adams advised.

- Parents set an example by being a good citizen.

- Be active in your child's school. The squeaky wheel gets the grease.

- Praise teachers and principals who are teaching our founding principles and history. Remember, by law, schools receiving federal funds are supposed to teach about the Constitution every year on September 17th.

- Help establish patriot clubs in your neighborhood. Encourage participation in patriotic activities along with sports and the arts.

- Light the fire in your child's mind about how great this country is through knowledge about our country.

- Don't be afraid of be part of a faction—the Founders wanted that to keep us strong.

- Being a patriot empowers children and creates active citizens, not victims. It develops leaders, and doesn't allow for apathy.

SUMMARY

The central theme of this book is that we must teach our children about their own sovereignty and their own responsibility to develop, in themselves, a love for this country. No one can do this for them. No one is going to make this happen; it is up to our children, on their own, to be patriots. They must understand the phrase "We the People" includes them too.

To be good patriots, they must:

- Learn the history.

- Have faith.

- Be good citizens.

- Do their civic duty.

- Pass these actions along to friends so others will be encouraged to show their patriotism as well.

Here are the bullet points from each of the chapters in one location as an "action item" list for parents to use when thinking about how they would like to raise their children as patriots.

Similar points have been consolidated. For example, almost every participant mentioned visiting historic sites as a family. Many also mentioned having dinner-time discussions with your children, voting and being good citizens, teaching about our history, the founding principles and values, and about keeping God in the discussion about how our country came to be.

I hope you found this book interesting and educational and that you find this list helpful in the raising of your own American patriots.

Key Points:

- Encourage your children to seek truth, not just a perception of truth, by looking at all sides of an issue, and by getting outside of themselves. This is the key to understanding anything in life, not just in being a patriot.

- Claims of justice—right and wrong—are critically important to examine to recognize one's values.

- Teach your children how to think critically for themselves so they can make their own educated decisions and not be led by others. Encourage them to think through *why* they hold their opinion, *then* share your opinion. Don't tell them what to think because they won't own their own opinions. Encourage them not to be afraid of be part of a faction—the Founders wanted that to keep us strong.

- God must be recognized as the cornerstone of our country's founding. Faith was an underlying component of our country's founding. The Founders had faith. Don't let God be taken out of the equation. The presence of a greater power than us is essential in understanding our nation and its destiny. Stand up for that—defend it to show your kids how to stand up for their beliefs. God gives us the faith to persevere. Make sure your children understand this intrinsically. Stress to your children that God gave us our rights, not the government.

- Per Jefferson and Madison, read the story of the country. Tell stories to your kids—make history interesting. By reading the original source documents together, you can instill a love for this country and illustrate the struggles and risks our Founders took so that we could have what we have today. Focus on the Founding Fathers and our early history, not the history of the special groups. Talk about the country's history and the blessings of freedom your children reap today because of that history.

- It is never too early to start talking about our country and its history. Talk about the flag, our presidents, and our freedoms. Talk about why certain people are on the money as an introduction to your children about the presidents.

- Teach your children about our founding principles and founding fathers, and let them repeat what they have learned so you can hear how they grasped a concept. Rote memorization won't stick with them. Tell stories to make it interesting. Read the Constitution and other important documents, and make this a part of your daily family discourse daily. Make sure they learn the Bill of Rights, the Amendments and how our government is structured. Read the Hillsdale *Constitution Reader* and the Declaration of Independence with your children and discuss.

- Light the fire in your child's mind about how great this country is through knowledge about our country.

- Remember RAPPS for the First Amendment (Freedom of Religion, Assembly, Press, Petition and Speech).

- Think enough each day, as John Adams advised.

- Learn the REAL history, especially of the historical figures who were minorities so all American kids can be proud of their county.

- It's very powerful when children understand this country's history and relate it to their own lives.

- Read historical fiction and non-fiction with your children.

- Be creative in how you teach kids about the country—try to use the 5 senses to reinforce learning. Make history fun. Put on a play about the Founders. Watch the musical *1776* with your children. Go to museums. Encourage them to join the debate team.

- Tell stories of your family history and the country's history to help them see the value of hard work, perseverance and internal fortitude. Learn about your family's heritage, where they came from, what was important to them and why. The stories will have a strong effect on your children. Visit where your ancestors are from in the country for a bigger impact.

- Consider making a book about your family's values and philosophy, mission statement, rules and goals, and include your photographs for a historical record. If you don't have any of ideas or traditions, start some.

- Find a trusted mentor for your child, a third party voice to be an influence. Also utilize other family members beyond parents like aunts and uncles.

- Teach your children politics cannot be ignored; it's a duty as a citizen to pay attention.

- Talk to your children about current events around the dinner table. Discussing current events helps your children stay aware and teaches them how to question if something sounds right or not in the media.

- Don't underestimate what your kids will understand. Discussions with your children may take longer than with an adult but remember how effective it is for a child to think through ideas on their own.

- Teach children to appreciate the freedoms they have in this country as compared to other countries. Talk to your children about how the United States allows for equal opportunity that other places don't. Freedom is the backbone of this nation— teach your kids to fight for their freedom.

- Don't be afraid to show your pride in our country—it rubs off on your kids. Encourage them to defend the greatness of this country and actively promote it. Be proud to be American. Have pride in your country and be proactive in showing this pride. Remind your children that America is the best place on Earth.

- Remember you don't have to be born in America to be a patriot.

- Keep in mind we must preserve America's sovereignty by fighting against the notion of globalism. God wants us to be independent nations, not one world government, according to the Book of Genesis. We are in a fight against what has become the new norm of global thinking. We must stand up for ourselves and our nation for our children's sake.

- Teach your children about perseverance and character. Even though it might not be easy to do something, sticking to it definitely has its rewards. Teach your children real values— honesty, love of country, duty. Consider giving your kids allowance as a way to teach them the value of money and about how to make their own decisions about things they want.

- Discuss how serving our country as a public servant is a very difficult and yet, rewarding job.

- Be a role model as our duty as citizens. We must vote and stand up for what we believe in, regardless of the outcome. It's the principle that counts, but be strategic in your choices. Voting is a responsibility.

- Participate in government in some way. This illustrates to your children your commitment to the country. Teach your children the duty of citizenship which includes voting, serving in public office or at least know what's going on in government and the community.

- Be active in your child's school. The squeaky wheel gets the grease. Praise teachers and principals who are teaching our founding principles and history.

- Remember how much influence you can have on your children and how they think about things. When you shake a veteran's hand and say "thank you," you are illustrating to your kids what respect and honor look like.

- Honor our veterans on Veteran's Day and Memorial Day.

- The warrior spirit is born in some people and cannot be denied. Help foster that in your children. Remember patriotism has many faces—citizen, soldier, and warrior.

- Remind your children that our freedom is not free. Talk about how our soldiers fight for our country and our freedoms and also fight for the freedoms of people in other countries. Visit military sites and talk about how soldiers keep us safe.

- Visit historical sites as a family such as Washington, DC, Philadelphia, PA, Williamsburg, VA and specific places such as Independence Hall, Monticello and Mount Vernon. Make it part of your vacation plans.

- Go to patriotic events such as Fourth of July parades and other community events and talk about why we celebrate our great country. Take your child to see the President if he (or she) visits your area. These experiences make it more tactile and effective for a child.

- Fly the American flag. Talk about its history and why you are proud to display it.

- Encourage your children to attend mock Congress camps and seminars to learn how government operates. Consider Junior Statesman programs, Boy Scouts and Girl Scouts, and The Young America's Foundation's programs for your children. Check out the Sea Cadet program for real life military experience. Help establish patriot clubs in your neighborhood. Encourage participation in patriotic activities along with sports and the arts.

- Challenge them to act on what they've learned about being a patriot such as babysitting for a military family, cook dinner for a military family or put together care packages for the troops.

- Get children involved in their community government for first-hand experience. Have your children take action—vote, volunteer, start something that doesn't already exist, let them see the amazing opportunities taking the initiative can offer a child.

- Encourage your children to rally their friends and take action even if it is not the "popular" idea—encourage them to stand up for their values. Debate is good—it is part of the foundation of our country. Don't let your children feel intimidated by the possibility of having a debate.

- Listen to what your children say to you and their friends about how they feel about our country and important issues and discuss these things with them.

- Teach your children that being a patriot empowers children and creates active citizens, not victims. It develops leaders, and doesn't allow for apathy.

ADDITIONAL RESOURCES

CHAPTER 1—Dr. Larry Arnn, president of Hillsdale College
(www.hillsdale.edu). Hillsdale College publishes a free monthly
publication called *Imprimis* which highlights recent lectures given at
Hillsdale. He is also the author of *Liberty and Learning: The Evolution of
American Education*, published by Hillsdale College Press in 2004, ISBN
978-0916308001.

CHAPTER 2—Rachel Campos- Duffy, author of *Stay Home, Stay
Happy- 10 Secrets to Loving At-Home Motherhood*, published by
Celebra Trade, August 25, 2009, ISBN 978-0451228079. She is also a
contributor to AOL. Her website is www.rachelcamposduffy.com.

CHAPTER 3—Rev. Steven Craft, founder of
www.christiancitizenshipministries.com and co-author with Roxon
Flowers of *Virtue and Vice: A Fascinating Journey into Spiritual
Transformation*, published by Christian Services Network, May 2005,
ISBN 9781593521158 and the author of *Morality and Freedom: America's*

Dynamic Duo (self-published through Author Solutions). He is also a speaker for the John Birch Society (www.jbs.org).

CHAPTER 4—Jackie Gingrich Cushman, author of *The Essential American: 25 Documents and Speeches Every American Should Own,* published by Regnery Press, November 23, 2010, ISBN 978-1596986435. She also co-authored *5 Principles for a Successful Life: From Our Family to Yours* with her father, Newt Gingrich, published by Crown Forum May 12, 2009, ISBN 978-0307462329. She writes for Townhall (www.townhall.com) and her website is www.jackiecushman.com. She mentions the book *A. Lincoln* by Ronald C. White, Jr., published by Random House Trade Paperbacks, May 4, 2010, ISBN 978-0812975703.

CHAPTER 5—Erick Erickson, editor of www.RedState.com and author of *Red State Uprising: How to Take Back America* published by Regnery Press, September 20, 2010, ISBN 978-1596986268. He mentions the book *1864: Lincoln at the Gates of History* by Charles Bracelen Flood, published by Simon & Schuster, February 16, 2010, ISBN 978-1416552291. He is also a contributor to CNN.

CHAPTER 6—Cathy Gillespie, co-chair for Constituting America (www.constitutingamerica.org), an organization dedicated to educating Americans about the founding documents and principles.

CHAPTER 7—Rick Green, speaker for Wallbuilders (www.wallbuilders.com) and founder of Patriot Academy (www.Patriotacademy.com) and Torch of Freedom Foundation (www.torchoffreedom.org). His website is www.rickgreen.com. In his interview, he mentions David Barton, the author of dozens of books available on the Wallbuilders website.

CHAPTER 8—Kevin Jackson, author of *The BIG Black Lie- How I Learned the Truth about the Democrat Party*, published by The Black Sphere (1ˢᵗ Edition), 2009, ISBN 978-0615302225. His website is www.theblacksphere.net.

CHAPTER 9—Debbie Lee, founder of America's Mighty Warriors (www.americasmightywarriors.org), an organization which helps care for the troops and their families and the families of the fallen warriors. Spokesperson for Move America Forward (www.moveamericaforward. org) and for the Tea Party Express (www.teapartyexpress.org). She also contributed to the book *Battlefields & Blessings: Stories of Faith and Courage from the War in Iraq and Afganistan*, published by AMG Publishers, November 11, 2009, ISBN 978-0899570419. It is available on Debbie's website store.

CHAPTER 10—Ed Meese, co-author of *The Heritage Guide to the Constitution (Regnery Publishing Inc, November 7, 2005, ISBN 978-1596980013), and Leadership, Ethics and Policing: Challenges for the 21st Century* (Prentice Hall, 2nd Edition, February 23, 2009, ISBN 978-0135154281); editor of *Making America Safer: What Citizens and their State and Local Officials Can Do to Combat Crime* (Heritage Foundation, February 1997, 978-0891950691); and author of *With Reagan: The Inside Story* (Regnery Gateway, June 28, 1992, ISBN 978-0895265227). The Heritage Foundation's website is www.heritage.org.

CHAPTER 11—Charlie Rhoads, a member of the board of directors for Joe Foss Institute (www.joefoss.com), a charitable organization which promotes patriotism, integrity and public service in addition to being the Chairman of the Board at America's Mighty Warriors (www. americasmightywarriors.com) which rights injustices and cares for the troops and their families and the families of the fallen. He has also been heavily involved with the Naval Special Warfare Foundation (www. nswfoundation.org).

CHAPTER 12 –Seth Swirsky, pop music songwriter and singer with two award-winning solo albums, *Watercolor Day* (2010) and *Instant Pleasure* (2004). He has written worldwide hits for numerous recording artists including Taylor Dayne ("Tell it to My Heart"), Al Green ("Love is a Beautiful Thing"), Celine Dion, Tina Turner and many others. He is also the author of three bestselling books that consist of handwritten letters from baseball players, including *Baseball Letters: A Fan's Correspondence with His Heroes* (Three Rivers Press, paperback edition, September 12, 2000, ISBN 978-0609807279), *Every Pitcher Tells A Story: Letters Gathered by a Devoted Baseball Fan* (Crown, 1st Edition, September 29,1999, ISBN 978-0812930559) and *Something to Write Home About: Great Baseball Memories in Letters to a Fan (*Random House, March 25, 2003, ISBN -10 0609608940). His documentary, *Beatles Stories* (2011), consists of stories told to him by people who have had an encounter with one or all of the "Fab Four". His website is www.seth.com.

Chapter 13—Janine Turner, author of *Holding Her Head High: 12 Single Mothers Who Championed Their Children and Changed History,* published by Thomas Nelson, March 4, 2008, ISBN 978-0785223245. She is the president and co-founder of Constituting America (www. constitutingamerica.org), an organization dedicated to educating Americans about the founding documents and principles. She is also a contributor to Politico (www.politico.com.) Her website is www. janineturner.com.

SUGGESTED READING

Documents and Books:

The Constitution

The Declaration of Independence and its amendments, including the Bill of Rights

The Federalist Papers—Alexander Hamilton, James Madison, John Jay

The Anti-Federalist Papers—Various authors

Imprimis—edited by Douglas A. Jeffrey, Hillsdale College

The Essential American: 25 Documents and Speeches Every American Should Own—Jackie Gingrich Cushman

The 5000 Year Leap: A Miracle That Changed the World—W. Cleon Skousen

The American Patriot's Almanac—William J. Bennett and John T.E. Cribb

The Heritage Guide to the Constitution —Edwin Meese, Matthew Spalding, and David F. Forte

A Patriot's History of the United States by Larry Schweikart and Michael Allen.

On-Line Resources:

The Founder's Constitution - http://press-pubs.uchicago.edu/founders/

The Brookings Institution: http://www.brookings.edu/topics/u-s-constitutional-issues.aspx

CATO Institute: http://www.cato.org/constitutional-studies

The Federalist Society: http://www.fed-soc.org/

Liberty Day: http://www.libertyday.org/

The Bill of Rights Institute: http://www.billofrightsinstitute.org/

The Heritage Foundation—First Principles http://www.heritage.org/Initiatives/First-Principles

The Allan P. Kirby, Jr. Center for Constitutional Studies and Citizenship of Hillsdale College http://www.hillsdale.edu/kirbycenter/

Hillsdale College Constitution Townhall—Free 5-Hour Seminar— "Reviving the Constitution" http://www.hillsdale.edu/KirbyCenter/programs/townhall/default.asp

Other:

Patriot Camp—http://patriotcamp.org/ located in Paxtang, Pennsylvania. Excellent resources for organizing short local summer camps promoting American history and patriotism.

Disclaimer: Inclusion of these resources here should not be seen as an endorsement by them of this book, the people in this book or the author.

FROM THE AUTHOR

I grew-up not thinking much about being an American. I knew I didn't want to leave America, and I liked being an American, but I didn't really know why. My parents didn't talk about politics because they were allied with different parties—my dad voted mostly Republican and my mom usually stuck with the Democrats.

Because I was a product of the media, I thought we did bad things, the Founding Fathers were selfish old guys and I don't remember ever reading the Constitution or even knowing what *The Federalist Papers* were as a young adult. I remember learning the Preamble of the Constitution by singing the song from *Schoolhouse Rock*, but I never thought about what the words really meant.

I voted singularly for candidates who voted pro-choice. They could have been Mao-loving Communists and I would have blindly voted on that one issue. I thought all guns were horrible and controlling those guns was the key to crime reduction, not thinking that criminals don't care about gun laws.

I didn't think about these things. I wasn't taught to THINK about them. Everyone I knew felt similarly, and it made me feel safe. I didn't think about the issues, our founding, how exceptional this country truly is, or God's role in all of this for a very long time, until the Spring of 2008, when I finally started reading the other side of issues as well.

In essence, I started really thinking and my eyes were opened. That awakening helped inspire me to write this book and I hope this book inspires you and your young patriots too.

The simple message is this: I'm just one of over 300 million Americans and I spoke to 13 other Americans, a tiny slice of who our patriots are. We are all Americans. We are all "We the People." This is our country; let's love it and teach our children to love it too.

For more information, additional resources, bulk orders, to share your patriotic story or to give feedback, check out the website www.raisinganamericanpatriot.com.

BUY A SHARE OF THE FUTURE IN YOUR COMMUNITY

These certificates make great holiday, graduation and birthday gifts that can be personalized with the recipient's name. The cost of one S.H.A.R.E. or one square foot is $54.17. The personalized certificate is suitable for framing and will state the number of shares purchased and the amount of each share, as well as the recipient's name. The home that you participate in "building" will last for many years and will continue to grow in value.

Here is a sample SHARE certificate:

YES, I WOULD LIKE TO HELP!

I support the work that Habitat for Humanity does and I want to be part of the excitement! As a donor, I will receive periodic updates on your construction activities but, more importantly, I know my gift will help a family in our community realize the dream of homeownership. **I would like to SHARE in your efforts against substandard housing in my community!** *(Please print below)*

PLEASE SEND ME _____ SHARES at $54.17 EACH = $ $_____

In Honor Of: _____

Occasion: (Circle One)   HOLIDAY   BIRTHDAY   ANNIVERSARY

        OTHER: _____

Address of Recipient: _____

Gift From: _____ *Donor Address:* _____

Donor Email: _____

I AM ENCLOSING A CHECK FOR $ $_____ PAYABLE TO HABITAT FOR HUMANITY OR PLEASE CHARGE MY VISA OR MASTERCARD *(CIRCLE ONE)*

Card Number _____ Expiration Date: _____

Name as it appears on Credit Card _____ Charge Amount $ _____

Signature _____

Billing Address _____

Telephone # Day _____ Eve _____

PLEASE NOTE: Your contribution is tax-deductible to the fullest extent allowed by law.
Habitat for Humanity • P.O. Box 1443 • Newport News, VA 23601 • 757-596-5553
www.HelpHabitatforHumanity.org

CPSIA information can be obtained at www.ICGtesting.com
Printed in the USA
237143LV00005B/2/P